A Dialogue on Consciousness

A Dialogue on Consciousness

Torin Alter
The University of Alabama
Robert J. Howell
Southern Methodist University

New York Oxford
OXFORD UNIVERSITY PRESS
2009

Oxford University Press, Inc., publishes works that further Oxford University's objective of excellence in research, scholarship, and education.

Oxford New York
Auckland Cape Town Dar es Salaam Hong Kong Karachi
Kuala Lumpur Madrid Melbourne Mexico City Nairobi
New Delhi Shanghai Taipei Toronto

With offices in
Argentina Austria Brazil Chile Czech Republic France Greece
Guatemala Hungary Italy Japan Poland Portugal Singapore
South Korea Switzerland Thailand Turkey Ukraine Vietnam

Published by Oxford University Press, Inc.
198 Madison Avenue, New York, New York 10016
http://www.oup.com

Library of Congress Cataloging-in-Publication Data

Alter, Torin Andrew, 1963-
A dialogue on consciousness/Torin Alter, Robert J. Howell.
p. cm.
Includes bibliographical references and index.
ISBN 978-0-19-537529-9 (pbk.) – ISBN 978-0-19-537530-5 (hardcover)
1. Consciousness. I. Howell, Robert. II. Title.
B105.C477A589 2009
126—dc22 2008028209

Printed in the United States of America
on acid-free paper

In loving memory of

Robert J. Howell Sr., Irving J. Alter, and Janet K. Alter

Contents

Preface

Melodies, images, and other conscious experiences populate our minds, both when we are awake and in dreams. Our heads, however, contain only a quiet, gray mass of brain tissue. How can this be? Despite mounting scientific evidence that consciousness results from brain activity, there is no getting around the sense of mystery that this proposition engenders. Can science explain not just the physical processes that underlie consciousness but consciousness itself? If not, then is consciousness nonphysical?

This dialogue explores these issues in depth. The characters debate the most significant theories and arguments in the field, including ideas from the Enlightenment to the present day. We have tried to present these ideas in an engaging and accessible way, without sacrificing rigor. We find them fascinating. We hope this book will lead others to feel similarly.

—T. A. & R. H.

Acknowledgments

We would like to thank Marion Alter, Russell Daw, Kyle Driggers, Joshua Ferris, John Heil, Holly Kennedy, Amy Kind, Alfred Mele, Matthew Price, and Brad Thompson for their many helpful stylistic and philosophical suggestions; David Chalmers, Jaegwon Kim, Derk Pereboom, and Ernest Sosa for their sage advice; Robert Miller for his enthusiasm and excellent editorial judgment; and the Philosophy Departments of Southern Methodist University and The University of Alabama. We also thank the many students, friends, and colleagues who have provided us with inspiration. Finally, we thank our families for their unfailing encouragement and support. We are particularly grateful to Lanie DeLay and to Elizabeth, Dora, and Irving Alter.

One philosopher's Modus Ponens is another philosopher's Modus Tollens.

—*Philosophical aphorism (origins unknown)*

Monday Night

Scene: Late night in the library. Two disheveled characters appear from the stairwell and move stealthily to an alcove between carrels, somewhere between Dewey Decimal 110 and 127. They are carrying seat cushions purloined from the Student Lounge. The less clean of the two holds his nose.

TOLLENS: Is it safe?

PONENS: (Sniffs) I think so. I think we can sleep here. It doesn't smell, and it's the philosophy section, so no one will be around.

TOLLENS: Thank God. I'm exhausted. I thought I was going to suffocate in the basement. What died in the air vents?

PONENS: Something. I don't even want to speculate.

TOLLENS: That's a first.

PONENS: Hey, I might be a philosophy student, but that doesn't mean I want to reflect on sour smells.

TOLLENS: You thought that was sour? Funny. I thought it was sort of pungently sweet. Awful all the same.

PONENS: I'm not surprised that a law student finds that sweet. No doubt it's sweet compared to the deeds lawyers contemplate on a daily basis.

TOLLENS: Cute. Keep the lawyer jokes coming. In a few years I'll laugh all the way to the bank.

PONENS: And I'll probably be flipping burgers.

TOLLENS: Don't let them say philosophy doesn't prepare you for something. In any case, I still say the smell downstairs was pungently sweet.

PONENS: Well, let's not argue. It's all subjective anyway.

TOLLENS: What do you mean, "It's all subjective"? It's not just a matter of opinion. If you said the air vent smelled like roses, or that it had no smell at all, you'd be wrong.

PONENS: Okay, fair enough. What I meant was that, although there's an objective fact about whether there are certain chemicals in the air, the way those chemicals smell is a matter of how the mind perceives them. Your mind might perceive them one way and mine another—the odor may be the same, if we're talking about the odorant molecules, but what it's like for us to smell it might differ.

TOLLENS: I don't know about that. For example, I wish you'd put your shoes back on. Your feet, I think, are objectively foul.

PONENS: Sorry.

TOLLENS: I'm not sure we disagree, but I'd be inclined to say that how we perceive odors has got to be an objective matter. It's just a matter of how information is processed in your brain. If I knew enough about your brain, I'd know how things smell to you.

PONENS: I'm not so sure about that. Does the state of my brain explain what it's like for me to smell the odor in the vent?

TOLLENS: Sure! Granted, neuroscience is far from complete, but it's all there in your brain.

PONENS: I don't have any doubt that the olfactory information is registered up there. But I deny that neuroscience explains consciousness. There's more to conscious experience than what neuroscience can reveal.

TOLLENS: Oh no, you're not telling me you think there's an immaterial soul! A ghost hanging about in your body smelling the smells!

Ponens and Tollens are startled by a grumble a couple of aisles over.

PONENS: Hello?

A scruffy character peers out from somewhere around the 200s.

TOLLENS: Well I'll be. Old Jimmy Nous! I thought you'd graduated!

NOUS: Just about. I have a few more credits to go.

TOLLENS: You living in the library too?

NOUS: Yep, got evicted earlier this month. I was sleeping in the science library but it was way too cold. Did I hear you guys arguing about the soul?

TOLLENS: Well, kinda. Ponens and I were just arguing about whether neuroscience can explain everything about the mind. He said it can't. Have I got you right, Ponens?

PONENS: Yes. But I didn't say anything about souls.

NOUS: Maybe you didn't, but I will. Souls definitely exist. They're what make us who we are!

TOLLENS: And during your last breath yours will no doubt exit your body through your lips, grow a pair of wings, and begin playing the harp on a cumulous cloud!

NOUS: Mock me if you want but, yeah, I believe in the eternal soul. The brain might be the mind, but that doesn't mean we don't have souls.

PONENS & TOLLENS: Hmmm.

PONENS: I'm not sure you want to say that.

NOUS: Why not? It's what I believe.

PONENS: I'm not saying you shouldn't believe in souls. I just think that if you believe in them, then you shouldn't believe the brain is the mind. You think your soul will survive the death of your body, right?

NOUS: I do.

PONENS: And your brain won't? It'll go into a coffin and rot with the rest of your body?

NOUS: Eventually. Unless I donate it to science.

TOLLENS: I wouldn't bother if I were you.

PONENS: Ignore Tollens. So, Nous, if your mind is the same thing as your brain, then apparently your mind rots when you die. That leaves your soul in a tough spot. Assuming it's your mind that thinks, feels, constitutes your character, has emotions, and all that, your soul is left rather, well, empty.

NOUS: Maybe I'll be different after I die, but it'll still be me.

PONENS: No, you see, that's just it. It seems that all of the things that make you who you are involve the mind. Memories are stored in the mind, right?

NOUS: Yeah.

PONENS: So if your mind is your brain, and you can't take your brain to heaven, you're not only going to lack emotions, beliefs, and a character—you're not going to have any memories, either.

TOLLENS: That doesn't sound like an afterlife much worth having, does it?

NOUS: I guess not. But you're not going to convince me to give up on a soul.

PONENS: I won't try to. I just want to convince you that when you're talking about the soul you're really talking about the mind. Perhaps an eternal mind, but a mind nonetheless.

NOUS: Okay, fair enough. I'm going to catch a little shut-eye over here, though, so . . .

TOLLENS: Wait now, Nous. You don't get out of the discussion that easily. Maybe Ponens won't try to convince you that there aren't any souls, but I will! There's absolutely no reason to believe in them! You yourself started out by saying that the brain is the mind, and you were right! What do you think that lump of oatmeal in your skull is doing if it isn't your mind? And if it's doing everything the neuroscientists say it is, why would you need a soul? A soul! Do you believe that nonsense, Ponens?

PONENS: Actually, I think you're being a little too quick . . . not to mention obnoxious. There are some interesting arguments for the existence of souls. The best-known argument was advanced by René Descartes in the seventeenth century.

TOLLENS: Ah, leave it to a philosopher to find salvation in a dead Frenchman.

PONENS: A very smart Frenchman, who . . .

NOUS: Did you know he had a thing for cross-eyed women?

Ponens and Tollens stare blankly for a few seconds.

TOLLENS: What?

NOUS: It's true. I read it in the *Encyclopedia Britannica.* He had a fetish.

TOLLENS: Maybe he just liked women who were fond of introspection.

NOUS: No, see he had a cousin . . .

PONENS: Okay, okay, I'm not sure I want to hear about it. Anyway, he gave an influential argument for the existence of souls. The book is around here somewhere. . . .

Ponens disappears into the stacks and returns shortly with a crusty old volume.

PONENS: Here's the relevant passage from Descartes' *Meditations on First Philosophy:*

> . . . I know that everything which I clearly and distinctly understand is capable of being created by God so as to correspond exactly with my understanding of it. Hence the fact that I can clearly and distinctly understand one thing apart from another is enough to make me certain that the two things are distinct, since they are capable of being separated, at least by God. The question of what kind of power is required to bring about such a separation does not affect the judgment that the two things are distinct. Thus, simply by knowing that I exist and seeing at the same time that absolutely nothing else belongs to my nature or essence except that I am a thinking thing, I can infer correctly that my essence consists solely in the fact that I am a thinking thing. It is true that I may have . . . a body that is very closely joined to me. But nevertheless, on the one hand I have a clear and distinct idea of myself, in so far as I am simply a thinking, non-extended thing; and on the other hand I have a distinct idea of body, in so far as this is simply an extended, non-thinking thing. And accordingly, it is certain that I am really distinct from my body, and can exist without it.

NOUS: Okay. Let's see. . . . I got very little from that.

TOLLENS: I must admit I'm with you there. I'm not sure where this God stuff comes in.

PONENS: Well, it's better in context.

NOUS: Do you mean after five or six beers?

PONENS: Look, the basic idea is pretty straightforward. Descartes conceives of his mind existing without his body and his body existing without his mind. He thinks that's pretty easy to do. The argument doesn't require you to believe in God, but it might be helpful to think about it that way. If God exists, he or she can do anything you can imagine. If you can imagine your body existing without your mind, or your mind existing without your body, then God can make it so. So, Descartes reasons, since God can separate your mind from your body, they're separable and thus distinct. You can't separate a thing from itself, after all.

NOUS: So there's proof? Descartes shows that souls exist?

PONENS: If his argument succeeds, his mind can exist without his body, including his brain. His mind could conceivably survive the total annihilation of his body and brain. Sounds like a soul to me.

NOUS: Right on!

TOLLENS: Sounds like sophistry to me.

PONENS: Well, let me make the argument a little clearer. Here, I'll write out the main steps:

Descartes' conceivability argument

1. I can clearly and distinctly conceive of my mind existing without my body and my body existing without my mind.
2. If I can clearly and distinctly conceive of X existing without Y and Y existing without X, then X can exist without Y and Y can exist without X.
3. Therefore, my mind and body can exist without each other.
4. Therefore, my mind and body are distinct.

PONENS: If Descartes' argument works, it generalizes in two ways. First, he could apply it not just to *his* body but to any body and indeed to any physical entity. If his reasoning is sound, his mind is distinct and separable from anything physical. Second, any reflective person should be able to apply the argument to his or her own mind and body. So, what do you think?

TOLLENS: The reasoning is clear enough, I suppose. But I'm not convinced. Maybe I'm not as imaginative as Descartes, but how am I supposed to imagine my mind without my body or my body without my mind?

NOUS: I don't find either so hard, but the second is especially easy; it's child's play to imagine your body existing without your mind.

TOLLENS: Oh? Enlighten me.

NOUS: One day you'll die and be a corpse. There's your body in the coffin, without your mind.

TOLLENS: Hmmm.

PONENS: That'll do for one part. For the other, just imagine this. You're lying in your bed, staring at the ceiling. You begin to feel yourself slowly rising. It feels like you're levitating above the bed.

TOLLENS: I think I might have experienced this.

PONENS: I don't doubt it. So you're levitating, and your perspective rotates to the point that you're looking back down at your body, apparently still on the bed. Then, your body just suddenly disappears. Poof! And you have the sense of floating around the room. You have no legs, no arms, nothing. You're just a mind with a field of vision.

TOLLENS: I haven't experienced that.

PONENS: I'm glad to hear it. You can imagine it though, can't you?

TOLLENS: Well, maybe, but . . . Wait! What am I seeing with? My eyes went poof too, right?

PONENS: Yeah, your eyes poofed, but you're not seeing with your eyes.

TOLLENS: Well that's quite a trick!

PONENS: I should say, rather, that you're not seeing at all. Rather, you're having a vision of the world.

TOLLENS: Ummm . . .

NOUS: Yeah, you know, like when you're dreaming. You can see things in your dreams when your eyes are closed, can't you?

PONENS: Right. There you go. Imagine the same thing, only it's not a dream.

TOLLENS: Ummm . . .

PONENS: Okay, if that doesn't work for you, just imagine that as you lift from your body, everything goes dark except for things that you're thinking. You might think, "What's going on here?" Eventually, you might find yourself thinking only about geometry problems.

TOLLENS: I doubt that, but okay. Let's say I can imagine this. What about premise 2? Why think that just because I can *imagine* my mind and body existing separately, they'll do so?

PONENS: Premise 2 doesn't have that implication. The conclusion says only that your mind and body *can* come apart. If you believe in an afterlife, perhaps you think they'll come apart after bodily death. But you could just as easily believe that they won't. You might say, just as there aren't any creatures with hearts but no kidneys—though it's not impossible—there aren't any creatures with minds but no bodies, though there could be.

NOUS: This brings us back to the idea that God can do anything we can imagine, right? It's not a particular point about souls and bodies.

PONENS: That's right, the point is general: Whatever is clearly conceivable is possible. And again, you don't have to be a theist to accept that principle.

TOLLENS: Ah, so that explains why you philosophers are always talking about crazy science-fiction scenarios. If imagination gives us insight into possibility, then imagination is a pretty powerful tool.

PONENS: Exactly. And this isn't something only philosophers do. Consider skiing.

TOLLENS: Skiing?

PONENS: Yes, on snow. Skiing is dangerous, and people who ski know this. They know they could break a leg, say. Yet they ski anyway.

NOUS: Not me. I'd never ski. I might break my leg!

PONENS: Okay, you might be afraid of breaking a leg, but you're not as afraid as you would be if you thought you couldn't survive a broken leg. That's because you know that you can exist without a leg.

TOLLENS: Okay.

PONENS: Well, how do you know that you can exist without a leg? You may never have broken it, and you certainly haven't had it amputated, so you haven't tested that idea experimentally. So how do you know?

NOUS: You imagine it!

PONENS: Right! It's enough for you to be able to *imagine* lacking your right leg and still hobbling along for you to realize you *can* survive without it—or as Descartes might have put it, your leg isn't an essential part of you.

TOLLENS: Yeah, but I can imagine myself putting on a cape and leaping tall buildings in a single bound. That doesn't mean that I can do it.

PONENS: Actually, doing that *is* possible in the broad sense I'm talking about. Your leaping over buildings is improbable, given the physical laws concerning gravity and such. But those laws could have been different. Under different physical laws, you'd be able to jump over buildings to your heart's content. Philosophers often call this "metaphysical" possibility as opposed to "natural" or "nomological" possibility, which is possibility given the laws of nature. Superheroic feats are metaphysically possible, even if in fact no superheroes exist.

NOUS: So really, anything is possible!

PONENS: No, some things are impossible even in the metaphysical sense. Even God couldn't make a round square or a monkey that's also a mud puddle. Such things are strictly impossible, to the point that their existence might even involve a contradiction.

TOLLENS: It's three in the morning, and we're talking about superheroes and mud-puddle monkeys. What's wrong with this picture?

NOUS: Yeah, it's time for a nap. I'm just going to doze here next to the Apocrypha if you don't mind. . . .

TOLLENS: But wait!

NOUS: Oh no.

TOLLENS: Superheroes! That's what's wrong with this!

PONENS: Maybe we should all go to sleep. I think you're getting a little loopy, Tollens.

TOLLENS: No, no. Listen. So Clark Kent is Superman, right? We all know that.

NOUS: Right.

TOLLENS: But Lois Lane doesn't know that. So she can imagine Clark Kent and Superman existing separately. She can imagine she's kissing Superman while a jealous Clark Kent looks on, or Clark Kent falling into Niagara Falls while Superman has a grand old time leaping over the Empire State Building. By Descartes' reasoning, we should conclude that such things are possible and that Clark Kent and Superman are distinct.

NOUS: But Lois Lane and Superman are fictional.

PONENS: No, Tollens is right about this.

NOUS: Look, I'm certain that at least Superman is fictional . . . isn't he?

PONENS: Yes, sorry. Lois Lane is fictional too. But that's not my point. My point is that this doesn't matter. Similar things happen all the time in real life.

NOUS: I thought you said no one actually jumps over buildings.

PONENS: Just listen, Nous. When I was a kid I had this annoying neighbor, Bernie Shucks. Bernie liked to shoot at squirrels with his air gun. I hated him. Then at a Halloween party I met this kid dressed up as Superman. We got along really well. We had a blast trick-or-treating together. Guess who that kid was? Bernie Shucks! I was in the same position as Lois Lane.

TOLLENS: So imagining something doesn't mean it's possible in any sense! While you were snagging Snickers bars with Superman, you might have been imagining Bernie Shucks sleeping in his bed, dreaming of vengeful rodents. This might have led you to conclude that your trick-or-treat buddy wasn't Bernie Shucks, even though he was. Perhaps Descartes was making a similar mistake when he drew a parallel conclusion about his mind and body based on what he could imagine.

PONENS: Yes, Descartes' argument had better not commit the Bernie Shucks fallacy. Actually, he was aware of that danger, sort of. Before publishing his *Meditations,* he passed the manuscript around to other great thinkers to elicit objections. Then he published the *Meditations,* the objections he received from those other thinkers, and his replies together in one big package. One of the objectors, Antoine Arnauld, voiced something like the Superman objection. He formulated the objection by imagining someone who thought he found a right-angled triangle with sides the squares of which don't equal the square of the hypotenuse. Here's what Arnauld said about this poor fellow:

> [If] he uses the same argument as that proposed by our illustrious author, he may appear to have confirmation of his false belief, as follows: "I clearly and distinctly perceive," he may say, "that the triangle is right-angled; but I doubt that the square on the hypotenuse is equal to the squares on the other two sides; therefore it does not belong to the essence of the triangle that the square on its hypotenuse is equal to the squares on the other sides."

TOLLENS: Nice example. So, he's saying that, although someone could conceive of a right triangle that doesn't conform to the Pythagorean Theorem, that doesn't mean there could be right triangles that violate the theorem. It means only that the person in question doesn't know his stuff when it comes to triangles.

PONENS: Right. And here Descartes can't complain that what the geometrically challenged person conceives is merely *naturally* impossible: It's mathematically impossible, and therefore metaphysically impossible, for there to be such a triangle.

NOUS: So Descartes' argument is bunk?

PONENS: No, that's too quick. Descartes had a ready answer, as Arnauld well knew: You can conceive of metaphysical impossibilities only if your conception is not, as Descartes put it, clear and distinct. The character in Arnauld's story isn't conceiving of triangles in a clear and distinct manner. Had that character been reasoning better, he would have seen that there could be no such triangle as the one he thought possible.

NOUS: Right! And Descartes should know a thing or two about good and bad geometrical reasoning. He invented analytic geometry, after all.

TOLLENS: Maybe so, but this is just cheating. How did Descartes know he was thinking clearly and distinctly when he imagined his mind existing without his body? He certainly didn't know everything about brains and bodies, and I doubt he knew everything there was to know about minds either. He was ripe for confusion! And so are we, for that matter!

PONENS: Yeah, that's what Arnauld said. The problem is widely regarded as the Achilles' heel of Descartes' argument. It's a dilemma, really. If the standards for thinking clearly and distinctly are high, we can't be sure we're thinking clearly and distinctly, and so we're not entitled to Descartes' first premise—the one about his conceiving his mind existing without his body and vice versa. But if the standards are low, then the second premise—the one that links conceivability and possibility—is subject to counterexamples such as Arnauld's.

NOUS: So now Descartes' argument is bunk?

TOLLENS: Looks like it, Nousy.

PONENS: Maybe it can be fixed. But the burden is on Descartes to defend the conceivability principle from Arnauld's dilemma.

NOUS: I'm not sure I can do that. Dang. I really wanted to believe in souls. My mother's going to be very annoyed with me.

PONENS: Hold on now, Nous. You shouldn't deny that souls exist just because one argument for their existence fails.

TOLLENS: But you *should* try to avoid believing things that are absurd.

NOUS: Absurd? Why is it absurd to believe in souls?

TOLLENS: The soul is a thing that doesn't exist in space but has your characteristics, drives, and thoughts, right?

NOUS: I'm not sure it doesn't exist in space.

TOLLENS: Then how big is it?

NOUS: Ummm . . .

TOLLENS: Bigger than a breadbox?

NOUS: Well, it's not like that. It doesn't have a three-dimensional shape.

TOLLENS: So it's two-dimensional, like a line? Is it circular or straight?

NOUS: I guess it's not two-dimensional either.

TOLLENS: So your soul is a geometrical point?

NOUS: Okay, so it's nonspatial.

TOLLENS: And this nonspatial thing has all your thoughts, memories, and everything mental?

NOUS: Sure.

TOLLENS: And since it's not in space, it's invisible.

NOUS: Well, you have to look inside.

TOLLENS: Careful you don't become like one of Descartes' favorite ladies.

NOUS: What?

PONENS: Ignore him, Nous. But look: Surely you grant that you can't see or hear souls . . .

NOUS: Right. That's why I said "look inside."

PONENS: But can you even introspect such a thing? Close your eyes and focus. You might detect your backache from sleeping on the floor, and you might detect a thought or two, but do you find some *entity* that's having those aches and thoughts?

NOUS: Hold on. Still looking.

PONENS: David Hume famously thought not, and many philosophers have come to agree with him. I grabbed his great work, *A Treatise of Human Nature,* when I was looking for Descartes' *Meditations*. Here's what Hume says:

> When I turn my reflexion on *myself,* I never can perceive this *self* without some one or more perceptions; nor can I ever perceive any thing but the perceptions. 'Tis the composition of these, therefore, which forms the self.

NOUS: That sounds kinda like what Buddhists report about meditation.

PONENS: Right. I think Hume would have agreed with them about the self.

NOUS: But just because you can't find something doesn't mean it's not there.

TOLLENS: Look out behind you! It's a rhinoceros!

Terrified, Nous spins around, and then slowly looks back.

NOUS: I don't see . . . Okay, I get your point. But still, one can have *faith* that there's a soul.

PONENS: You're right, and remember, someone might come along and bolster Descartes' argument, in which case you wouldn't have to rely on faith. But there are other problems with believing in souls.

NOUS: Great. Mother's going to be really displeased.

TOLLENS: Something tells me she already is. Does she know you sleep in libraries?

PONENS: Ignore Tollens, Nous. One problem was raised by Princess Elizabeth of Bohemia, in her correspondence with Descartes.

TOLLENS: A member of a royal family did serious philosophy? Really?

PONENS: It's true. She was quite sharp, actually. Here's her criticism, in a nutshell: If souls are nonspatial, they don't seem capable of doing the pushing and pulling that is expected of them.

NOUS: Pushing? Pulling?

PONENS: Whatever else is true of the mind, it interacts in significant ways with the body. Your desire to hail a taxi causes you to raise your arms. And your being hit by a cab causes you to feel enormous pain and to want to go to the hospital. Sound vibrations coming from my vocal chords and impinging on your ear drums cause you to have new thoughts. So, bodily phenomena, such as brain states, ear-drum vibrations, and behavior, cause mental phenomena, such as pains, desires, and thoughts; and mental phenomena cause bodily phenomena. To deny those claims would be to deprive the soul of any significant connection to the physical world.

NOUS: Okay. But why think it can't push and pull?

TOLLENS: I see the Princess' point. Do you see the restrooms at the end of the stacks? Suppose I told you to flush the toilet in the women's room without leaving the men's room. How would you do it?

NOUS: I don't know. I guess I couldn't.

TOLLENS: Right, because to do so, you have to enter the space where the action is to be performed. You have to be there to pull the plunger.

NOUS: Ah, no, I have it. I could rig up a string tied to the plunger, and pull it from the men's room!

TOLLENS: You're missing the point. You still have to have spatial contact with something that has spatial contact with the plunger, and that requires you to be in space. But the soul isn't in space at all! It can't be pulling three-dimensional strings! Because it's *spatially* isolated from physical things, it's *causally* isolated from those things.

NOUS: I see. Pushing and pulling involve occupying and moving in space. So, since the soul doesn't occupy or move in space, it can't push or pull.

TOLLENS: By Jove, I think he's got it!

NOUS: But what about remote control? Some toilets, you know, have those laser thingies that flush when you walk away from them. You don't even have to touch the handle. Doesn't that mean that not all causing is pushing and pulling?

PONENS: And don't forget about magnets.

NOUS: How do you flush a toilet with a magnet?

TOLLENS: I think he means that magnetic fields don't require the sort of physical contact that pushing and pulling requires.

NOUS: Ah, right.

PONENS: Yes, as I first stated it, the pushing-and-pulling objection assumes what's sometimes called contact mechanics. Action at a distance was strongly rejected by many, at least until Newton.

TOLLENS: But the basic problem remains. Even action at a distance requires spatial location for both the actor and the thing acted upon. It's action at a *distance,* after all, and only two things existing in space can be at a distance from one another. Magnetic fields and other such things have spatial extent, so even here our conception of causation is closely intertwined with spatial location.

PONENS: Right. This is a problem for anyone who believes in souls. Wanting there to be entities that are nonphysical and yet causally connected to the physical world is seen as wanting to have your cake and eat it too.

TOLLENS: Mmmm. Soul cake.

NOUS: I admit this is troubling. But just because all the causation we've discovered involves only physical phenomena doesn't mean that souls can't cause things to happen in the physical world.

TOLLENS: Go ahead, believe in magic. I'm not stopping you.

NOUS: Make fun. I don't care.

PONENS: He is making fun, Nous, but he has a point. Any such causation would be so different from the way we conceive of causation as to almost warrant the term "magic."

NOUS: Why?

PONENS: Because spatial relations are intertwined with our concept of physical causation. If you're playing pool, you can tell which ball hit the eight ball by looking at their spatial positioning. Suppose there are two souls, Tweedledee and Tweedledum, and one body. Both Tweedledee and Tweedledum want to raise the body's arm. Suppose the arm is raised. Which soul did it? You can't say it was the soul in the body because being *in* something is a spatial notion. The same point holds for being *near* something, being *next to* something, and so on. The problem is, unless souls are spatial, there are no grounds for saying that one soul rather than the other causes the arm to move. You see, Nous, there's a problem about how a soul could even be linked to a particular body. Nous?

Nous snores and turns over in his sleep.

PONENS: Oh well.

TOLLENS: Poor soul is just worn out.

PONENS: Yeah, so's mine. Maybe we'd better call it a night.

TOLLENS: Yeah. I've got a big day tomorrow.

PONENS: Really? What do you have planned?

TOLLENS: Gotta wake up and then go to bed again.

PONENS: You're pitiful. Good night.

TOLLENS: 'Night.

Tuesday Night

Scene: In a dark corner of the library, Ponens and Tollens are sprawled, wearing clothes that would look strikingly familiar if dialogues were sitcoms. They are lying with their heads propped on pillows cobbled out of dusty books and folded overcoats.

TOLLENS: Where's Jimmy Nous? I haven't seen him around tonight.

PONENS: Big surprise. You weren't exactly the measure of manners last night.

TOLLENS: Ah, well. If you can't take the heat, get out of the stacks. At least we'll hear no more about souls.

PONENS: All views need defenders, I suppose.

TOLLENS: You know, I thought you'd be on his side. Weren't you going on about how neuroscience is limited—how it leaves out certain things about the mind?

PONENS: Yep.

TOLLENS: But if you don't believe in immaterial souls, then what do you think neuroscience leaves out?

PONENS: Why consciousness exists.

Ponens and Tollens hear a "Hah!" from the stacks, somewhere in the 500s.

PONENS: Excuse me? Is someone there?

A woman in a white coat suddenly rolls out from between the aisles on a wheeled stool. With a kick, she propels herself towards the corner occupied by Ponens and Tollens.

TOLLENS: Lo! Another after-hours denizen of the stacks!

BELLA: Name's Sarah. Sarah Bella. Pleased to make your acquaintance.

PONENS: I'm Ponens, this is Tollens.

BELLA: Are those last names or first names?

TOLLENS: Last.

BELLA: Why don't you use your first names?

PONENS: Our first names are the same: we're both Modus. It gets confusing.

TOLLENS: Funny we've never run into you before, Sarah. We're here often.

BELLA: By the distinctive scent you guys are cultivating in this corner, I'm not inclined to doubt you.

TOLLENS: Sorry. We would petition for showers in the Government Documents Room if we weren't here illegally.

BELLA: That's alright. I usually stay in the science library, but tonight I didn't make it before they locked the doors. Tell me, did I hear one of you speak disparagingly about neuroscience?

Tollens points at Ponens and makes swirling motions next to his ear.

PONENS: I wasn't speaking against neuroscience or any other science for that matter. I was saying only that the objective, physical sciences are limited in what they can tell us about consciousness.

BELLA: Consciousness. Hmmm. I'm not sure what you mean by that. If you're talking about cognition, I don't see why science leaves anything out. In fact, scientists have already built thinking machines. They're called *computers*. In 1997, Deep Blue beat Garry Kasparov, the best chess player in human history. And Deep Blue doesn't hold a candle to programs developed more recently. There are programs that compose original music, compositions that even experts can't distinguish from unknown masterpieces created by emotionally overwrought composers. Video games include "bots" that can reason, talk, remember, and pretty much destroy regular human players, and . . .

TOLLENS: Whoa, Nellie! I think we get the picture. I know what you're talking about, but why aren't these computers just complicated nonconscious automata?

BELLA: Let's compare. These so-called automata play chess and write music. And you guys . . . what exactly do you do with your time, anyway?

PONENS & TOLLENS: Ummm . . .

BELLA: I'll bet in not too many years we'll look back on talk about "consciousness" as just so much noise, vented to preserve the sense that there's something special and unique about human minds. We'd do best just to get over it.

PONENS: I think there's something right in what you're saying, Sarah, but maybe we should go a little slower. There are a few distinctions . . .

TOLLENS: Oh no. Here we go with the distinctions.

PONENS: Well, I do want to distinguish between the baby and the bathwater, so both don't get thrown out.

BELLA: I have no idea what you are talking about. Who said anything about babies?

PONENS: It's just a figure of speech. I think we agree, more or less, about cognition—thinking, believing, reasoning, and so on. And I agree, science could develop thinking computers, if it hasn't already.

BELLA: Well there you go. What else is there?

PONENS: Consciousness! Think about the feeling of pain, the smell of a wet dog, or the visual sensation of redness. Each of those experiences has a distinctive felt quality. How could neuroscience explain why brain processes give rise to conscious experience at all, let alone experiences with those particular felt qualities?

TOLLENS: Why do you think there's such a big difference between thought and experience? If there's a real problem here, then why doesn't it also arise for explaining how the brain generates thought?

PONENS: Purely cognitive states concern information storage and processing. Unless the information is about consciousness, I see no compelling reason to doubt that cognitive science can fully explain how the mind stores and processes it. For example, linguists develop theories about how we parse sentences—how we do such things as identify the subject, object, and verb. And neuroscience investigates the underlying brain mechanisms.

TOLLENS: Whoa, they've figured all that out?

PONENS: No, not even close. But some aspects of how we understand and produce language are reasonably well understood, and headway is being made all the time. I see no reason why the methods used in cognitive science can't eventually explain how cognition works, without remainder.

TOLLENS: I still don't see why you're so confident. Maybe some aspects of cognition are easy to explain and others aren't.

PONENS: That's a fair point. Another example is mental representation—thinking *about* objects, as in perception. That's a pretty fundamental notion in cognitive sciences, and some philosophers argue that mental representation depends essentially on consciousness. That's controversial, but if it's correct perhaps cognitive science can't fully explain thought, either.

TOLLENS: Right.

PONENS: But if we set that issue aside, there's reason for optimism. Arguably, the nature of a cognitive state is determined primarily by its causal relations to behavior and to other cognitive states.

TOLLENS: You're losing me.

PONENS: Suppose someone says, "It's raining," grabs an umbrella before going outside, cancels her picnic plans, and thinks to herself, "The roads will be slippery if this keeps up." We have good reason to conclude that she believes it's raining, don't we?

TOLLENS: Obviously.

PONENS: Okay, and how can you tell whether someone has a strong desire to have a drink? Maybe you ask him. Or maybe you just notice that he gets weak knees when passing the local pub and that he quickly accepts a drink when one is offered. And why do we say my dog Fifi remembers me?

TOLLENS: Fifi?

PONENS: It's just a hypothetical example.

TOLLENS: But *Fifi*?

PONENS: Whatever. Anyway, why conclude that Fifi remembers me when I walk in the front door? Because she warms up to me quickly, wags her tail, and doesn't bark. And because she runs over to her food bowl, indicating a relationship between her remembering me, her desire for food, and her belief that I'll feed her.

TOLLENS: Okay, already. What's your point?

PONENS: That beliefs, desires, and other cognitive states are closely interconnected and that they're closely connected to behavior. If someone behaves in none of the ways typically associated with believing that it's raining and has none of the associated states, such as the belief that the ground is getting wet, we'd have ample reason not to attribute to her the belief that it's raining.

TOLLENS: So your point is about how we *know* about the cognitive states of others? It's a point about knowledge?

PONENS: No, I was trying to draw attention to something about the nature of cognition: A cognitive state's connections to behavior and to other cognitive states are central to the nature of that state. And the methods of cognitive science are well suited to explaining such connections. The states can be characterized in functional terms.

TOLLENS: Functional terms?

PONENS: Right: in terms of roles the states play in the cognitive life of the organism. Parts of cognitive science, such as psychology and linguistics, can explain those roles. Linguistic theories about how we parse sentences would be an example. Neuroscience, or perhaps neuroscience plus other sciences, can explain the underlying mechanisms—the brain states and processes that produce the relevant behavior. Such sciences can also explain connections among various states.

TOLLENS: Okay, I guess I see that if cognition consists in functional relations among states and behavior, then cognitive science could in principle explain how cognition works. But isn't consciousness also closely tied to behavior and to various cognitive states? We talked about this last night. Doesn't the sensation of pain tend to cause yelps, the tendency to avoid things that cause pain, and stuff like that?

PONENS: Suppose it does. But do such tendencies constitute what pain is? I think not. Pain, the felt quality, is something over and above its typical causes and effects and its relations to other mental states. Maybe cognitive states such as beliefs and desires can be completely explained in functional and physical terms. Once you've explained how such states store information and cause behavior you've pretty much said all there is to say about them. But I don't see how any characterization of this sort could capture what it's like to feel pain. Not only does pain tend to cause some states and be caused by others—it also feels like something.

BELLA: I think you probably have more than your share of confusion here, but let me just start by pointing out the most obvious mistake.

TOLLENS: Oooh! I'm liking the sound of this! No sleep tonight for Ponens!

BELLA: You have a confused notion of consciousness. To be conscious of something is just to be aware of it. As in "I am conscious of a musty smell in this corner of the library." But I assume you agree that computers can be aware of things. After all, the sliding doors in the supermarket open because they're aware that someone's in front of them, and the thermostat turns on the air-conditioning when it's aware that the science library gets above 55.

TOLLENS: 55?

BELLA: Scientists like it crisp.

PONENS: Sarah, I grant you that there's a sense of the term "consciousness" in which consciousness is just awareness of something. Thermostats, sliding doors, and computers are conscious in that sense. Computers can even be *self*-conscious in that sense, as when they monitor their own hard drives for errors. But your own examples suggest that there's another notion of consciousness. A thermometer registers the presence of molecular kinetic energy, but it has no experiences. It doesn't feel warm or cold. When a computer's microprocessor overheats, does it feel like a retiree who's been on the beach too long? Does it feel anything at all? Are its activities, including its self-monitoring activities, accompanied by felt experience? I doubt it.

BELLA: The difference here is just a matter of complexity. It's not a matter of some further kind of phenomenon, in addition to awareness.

PONENS: I think it *is* something further. Consider an example taken from the science books you love so dearly. Neuroscientists have discovered something they call "blind-sight."

TOLLENS: "Blind-sight" sounds like an oxymoron.

PONENS: But the condition is real. People with certain sorts of brain damage claim to be blind, but when prompted they show definite signs of receiving visual information—information that's not accompanied by the usual visual sensations. So, for example, when an experimenter holds a certain number of fingers before these people and asks them how many they see, they say they don't see anything. But if prompted to guess, they often get it right. They score significantly better than chance. In other experiments, the subjects are asked to point at locations of objects that the subjects insist they can't see. Once again, these people get the locations right a significant percentage of the time, despite insisting that they can't see a thing!

TOLLENS: And this proves . . .

PONENS: The conclusions are debatable, but many have taken the experiments to show that there can be visual awareness without visual experience. If that's right, then we should distinguish consciousness in the sense of awareness from consciousness in the sense of experience. And if the distinction is legitimate, then explaining how physical processes give rise to awareness wouldn't necessarily help explain how physical processes give rise to experience.

BELLA: I'd have to study the experiments.

PONENS: You don't trust me?

BELLA: I don't doubt that blind-sight exists. But the details may matter. Anyway, you yourself said that in such cases the impairment comes from brain damage. So, what the blind-sighters lack isn't some mysterious, nonphysical property. They have deficiencies that can be explained in purely neurological terms.

PONENS: That's right. I don't doubt that brain states underlie consciousness or that brain damage can result in the loss of the capacity for having conscious states. But it doesn't follow that neuroscience can fully explain why brain states are accompanied by subjective experience, let alone why they're accompanied by this or that kind of experience.

BELLA: I'm losing track of what you're saying, and I don't think it's my fault. I think I'll scoot back to my own aisle. . . .

PONENS: No hold on. I think I can make myself clearer.

TOLLENS: Yes, Sarah, please stick around! Don't leave me alone with a talkative philosopher!

BELLA: Alright. Bring on the clarity.

PONENS: One thing I've found helpful is an article by Thomas Nagel from the '70s called "What Is It Like to Be a Bat?"

TOLLENS: From the *'70s*? Yesterday we were talking about an argument Descartes gave in the seventeenth century, and now you're jumping ahead to the late twentieth century! What happened in between?

PONENS: Hmmm, let's see. Darwin wrote *The Origin of Species.* The Beatles played Shea Stadium. And I think there were a few wars.

TOLLENS: Ha, ha. You know what I'm getting at. Over those three centuries, weren't there developments that shed light on consciousness and the physical world?

PONENS: Of course! A ton happened during that period. But unless you want to be here all night . . .

TOLLENS: Well, I *am* going to be here all night.

BELLA: But I may not. Let's hear the quick version.

PONENS: Alright, the quick version. Before the Enlightenment, distinctions between physical phenomena and their effects on our minds were often blurred. For example, scholars in the Middle Ages tended to characterize temperature partly in psychological terms. Descartes and other Enlightenment figures took a new approach. They sought to describe the physical world in entirely nonmental, mechanical terms. Temperature was no longer understood even partly in terms of how it makes us feel. It was instead regarded as an entirely objective, physical phenomenon. This approach—detaching the workings of the physical world from those of the mind—helped enable knowledge to grow in the remarkable way it has ever since.

TOLLENS: Wait a minute. Did Descartes just ignore the way physical things affect our minds?

PONENS: No, but he relegated mental phenomena to a separate, nonphysical realm, which he distinguished sharply from the physical realm of extended matter. And he didn't think the objective approach he advocated for studying physical phenomena could apply to mental phenomena.

BELLA: Maybe he was wrong about that.

PONENS: Many believe he was. The objective approach led to so many advances in our understanding of the physical world that it was natural to try the same approach when it came to studying the mind. And this has been done. We find it in modern linguistics, modern psychology, and various other disciplines that fall under the heading of "cognitive science." As a result, we know a great deal about how the mind works—more, perhaps, than Descartes could have imagined.

BELLA: How shocking! Applying science to the mind actually helps us understand it!

PONENS: Yep, it seems obvious, and now just about everyone agrees. Some philosophers have taken the idea one step further. Not only is the mind well-suited for scientific investigation: The mind is just part of the world described by physics—just part of the physical world. That's a consequence of physicalism.

TOLLENS: Is physicalism the same as materialism?

PONENS: Right, same view. It says that everything, including mental phenomena, is physical. All information is physical information, all truths are physical truths, all properties are physical properties; the physical world is the whole world. This view is widely held, but it wasn't always. Rejecting it wasn't unusual in Descartes' day or for the three centuries that followed. But by around the middle of the twentieth century, physicalism had become the received view, at least in Anglo-American philosophy. It remains so today.

BELLA: As it should!

PONENS: Perhaps, but there's another side to the story. Descartes relegated the mind to a separate, nonphysical realm partly because it seemed recalcitrant to the objective, mechanistic approach. As John Locke put it, matter in motion, no matter how fast or complex, just couldn't explain the *sensation* of heat—why that sensation occurs or why it feels the way it does.

TOLLENS: Right.

PONENS: Many twentieth-century philosophers rejected Descartes' division of the world into separate physical and nonphysical realms. But this left the original problem unsolved. Whether the mind resides inside or outside the physical realm, it's hard to see how *subjective* experiences such as the sensation of heat could be fully explained in *objective,* physical terms. The "matter in motion" problem is still there.

BELLA: But no one says that the sensation of heat is just matter in motion—at least, not just any old matter in motion. Sensations are brain processes, which involve electrochemical changes.

PONENS: The same problem arises for the idea that sensations are brain processes.

BELLA: Why?

TOLLENS: I think what Ponens is saying is that when science turned its gaze to the mind, it maintained the assumption that everything can be explained in fully objective terms. That assumption was bound to create a problem for explaining consciousness because consciousness presents itself as an irreducibly *subjective* phenomenon. Descartes avoided the problem by placing the mental in a nonphysical realm and thereby removing consciousness from the purview of objective science. But physicalists, who reject his dualism, couldn't follow his lead. Eventually, they'd have to face the problem he and other Enlightenment figures set aside.

PONENS: Bingo. I think that's just what Nagel would say.

BELLA: And I think that argument seems right to you only because you're operating on such a general level. You're not really looking at the science.

PONENS: Hold on, I haven't explained Nagel's argument yet. I was just describing the historical background.

BELLA: Let's hear the argument, then. His article is called something or other about bats, right?

PONENS: "What Is It Like to Be a Bat?"

TOLLENS: Right. Why does he talk about bats?

PONENS: He points out that many bats have a way of sensing the world that we lack.

TOLLENS: Echolocation.

PONENS: Right. These bats use a sort of natural sonar. They emit high-pitched chirps and hear the sound waves bounce off objects. This enables the bats to locate those objects. It's how they navigate their way around their environment.

BELLA: Okay. So?

PONENS: So biology and neuroscience can explain a lot about bat echolocation: how the sound waves are emitted, how the bats receive and store the information about what the sound waves bounce off, and how the bats use that information to hunt mosquitoes and fly around trees. But there's something we can't discover in these ways. We can't discover what it's like for the bats to echolocate. We can't answer the title question of Nagel's article: "What Is It Like to Be a Bat?" Likewise, cognitive science might be able to explain how human cognition works and how we navigate our way to a candy store, but it won't be able to explain what it's like to taste chocolate—at least not using its standard methods.

TOLLENS: Hold on there, Ponens. Maybe knowing what parts of the bat's brain are used in processing echolocation information would help us understand what it's like to be a bat. For example, suppose we find that the parts correspond, to some extent, to our visual and auditory cortexes. That might support a hypothesis that echolocation feels similar to a combination of hearing and seeing.

PONENS: I doubt it's that simple. But even if the hypothesis you mention is true, consider how we'd come to know what it's like to echolocate. We'd start with experiences familiar to us—hearing and seeing—and try to imaginatively project ourselves into the bat's circumstances. We'd try to occupy its point of view.

TOLLENS: Why does that matter?

PONENS: Because then, to figure out what it's like to echolocate, we'd be relying on our own subjective experiences, not just objective science. Anyway, again, your hypothesis is questionable. Granted, I can imagine experiences I've never had. I've never tasted a pretzel with ketchup. Still, I bet I can imagine what it'd be like to taste that combination of flavors since I've tasted each individually. But not all cases work like that, and the bat case may be an exception. Nagel talks about bats because they experience the world in an unfamiliar way—too unfamiliar for us to imagine.

TOLLENS: How does he know that?

PONENS: He doesn't. He's making an educated guess, based on the behavioral and anatomical differences between bats and us. Anyway, there *could* be creatures that have conscious experiences that differ radically from any experiences we have, right?

TOLLENS: I suppose.

PONENS: Okay, so the question of whether bats fit the bill isn't so important here; if bats don't, then there could be other creatures that do. So, for the sake of argument, let's suppose echolocation is as Nagel believes it is: radically different from experiences we know firsthand.

TOLLENS: Okay.

PONENS: Well then, you can see why he doesn't think we can do the pretzel-with-ketchup trick for bat echolocation. We lack the experiential elements needed for adopting the bat's viewpoint. Our brain states are too different from theirs to do the imaginative projection.

TOLLENS: So . . .

PONENS: So, if we're ever going to know what it's like to be a bat, we're going to have to rely on objective science, not imagination. But objective science isn't up to the task. Studying bat brains objectively might tell us how bats process information about their environment, but it won't tell us what it's like for them to experience the world.

TOLLENS: So let's say you're correct about this.

BELLA: I'm not convinced. I'd have to study more about bat brains.

TOLLENS: Yeah, but granting your point, Ponens, what do you conclude from this?

PONENS: Well, it's part of why I'm not a physicalist. In other words, it's why I don't believe that the features revealed through physical science are the only features there are. Nagel's example illustrates what those sciences miss.

BELLA: I thought this was supposed to make things clearer. Nagel's reasoning seems just as soft-minded as anything you were saying before.

TOLLENS: Hold on Sarah, Nagel may be on to something. But you're right, the argument isn't yet clear. Ponens, why can't we accept his claims about our inability to know what it's like to be a bat while at the same time maintain that consciousness—including bat consciousness—is entirely physical?

PONENS: Perhaps you can, and Nagel recognizes that possibility. But there's a genuine problem for physicalism here. Nagel brings this out by comparing physicalism to the hypothesis that matter is energy. The truth of that hypothesis follows from modern physics. But what if you were a pre-Socratic philosopher, who knew nothing about modern physics? Take Thales . . .

TOLLENS: Thales?

PONENS: A philosopher who lived before Socrates and thought everything was water.

BELLA: Where did he live, in a well?

PONENS: No, but he did allegedly fall down a well once while walking around gazing at the stars.

TOLLENS: And so philosophy was born!

PONENS: That was apparently the joke at the time. But Thales wasn't crazy. He just lived in a different, scientifically unsophisticated time. So Nagel's question is, "Could Thales have understood the matter-is-energy hypothesis?"

TOLLENS: Well, he might have been able to understand what was being said, but his understanding would have been superficial. Hell, my understanding of that hypothesis is pretty superficial.

PONENS: Right. And the reason is that Thales, and perhaps you as well, lacked a theoretical framework that explains *how* matter and energy could be the same. Without such a framework, the hypothesis should seem mysterious.

TOLLENS: So Nagel thinks we're in a similar position with respect to physicalism?

PONENS: Yes.

TOLLENS: Why?

PONENS: Because of subjectivity. Phenomenal qualities—the qualities that constitute what it's like—are subjective. At least, they seem to be. To understand what it's like to be a bat, for example, it looks as though one must adopt the viewpoint of the bat, or at least a similar viewpoint. It's our inability to adopt such a viewpoint that explains why we can't understand what it's like for them to echolocate. But physical properties would appear to be objective, viewpoint independent. So, even if phenomenal properties are physical, seeing how this could be so would require having an appropriate theoretical framework. Presently, we lack such a framework. Neuroscience and chemistry don't supply it. All they seem to deliver is objective information. And it's hard to see how or even if such a framework could be constructed.

TOLLENS: Interesting. Could I summarize Nagel's reasoning like this?

Nagel's argument

1. We can understand how physicalism might be true only if we have a theoretical framework that explains how phenomenal properties, which seem subjective, might really be objective, physical properties.
2. We have no such framework.
3. Therefore, we cannot understand how physicalism might be true.

PONENS: You've got it.

TOLLENS: In that case, my earlier complaint stands. Suppose we don't understand how physicalism might be true, as Nagel's argument concludes. Even so, physicalism might be true and we might even have good evidence for its truth.

BELLA: I agree with Tollens. Nagel's argument doesn't make me think I should give up physicalism. At best, it makes me think we should do more science. I think Nagel underestimates the explanatory potential of the framework already provided by neuroscience.

PONENS: Maybe, though I doubt it. Impressive as it is, neuroscience still has a long way to go. But let's put Nagel's argument aside, at least for now. There's another argument that might bring the problem with physicalism into sharper relief.

BELLA: Sharpen away.

PONENS: Imagine a time far in the future when the science of color vision has been completed. And imagine Sarah has a brilliant cousin named Mary.

BELLA: How did you know about my cousin Mary? She's the Scrabble champion of North Dakota!

TOLLENS: I'm glad all that intelligence isn't being wasted.

PONENS: Okay, so maybe it's not your cousin Mary, but another Mary. Mary is a brilliant scientist who has spent her life locked in a black-and-white room.

BELLA: So how did she become so well educated?

PONENS: She was taught everything through lectures on black-and-white television—or maybe black-and-white podcast lectures. In this way, she learns the completed science of color vision. In fact, let's suppose she learns the complete physical truth—all physical facts.

TOLLENS: Physical facts?

PONENS: Yes, physical facts. You're asking for a definition of "physical"? I won't try to give you one. The notion of the physical is notoriously hard to define. But the basic idea is pretty straightforward. Frank Jackson says something useful about this.

TOLLENS: Who?

PONENS: He came up with the Mary case. I have his article here.

TOLLENS: What, you just carry it around?

PONENS: It's a classic! And I thought it might come in handy. Here's the relevant passage:

> [Mary] knows all the physical facts about us and our environment, in a wide sense of "physical" which includes everything in completed physics, chemistry, and neurophysiology, and all there is to know about the causal and relational facts consequent upon all this, including of course functional roles.

TOLLENS: Okay, that's pretty clear. Mary knows everything one could know through completed physics, chemistry, and neuroscience—everything about how roses reflect light, how the visual cortex works, and so on.

PONENS: We also have to assume that she knows everything that follows logically from her scientific knowledge, including information about the causes and effects of color experience.

TOLLENS: Okay.

PONENS: Then one day her captors release her from the black-and-white room and present her with a red rose.

TOLLENS: Oh, how sweet! That will certainly make up for a lifetime of imprisonment.

PONENS: Maybe not, but the point is that when she sees red for the first time, she learns something new. She finally understands *what it's like* to see red.

TOLLENS: That seems right. It's likely to be quite a revelation for her. It'll probably only make her angrier about being cooped up in a cell all that time, though. I can just hear her. "You've kept me locked up like this when there are red things out there! You bastard!"

PONENS: Well, not quite. She knew there were red things out there. She also knew that red things reflect light in certain ways, that some roses are red, and that women swoon when given roses.

BELLA: You don't know much about women, do you?

PONENS: Not really. Anyway, when she leaves the room she learns something new—something about the color experiences those outside the room were enjoying while she was studying in black and white. Before leaving, she learned everything about the structure, function and composition of their brains. Only after leaving does she learn that when their brains were in a certain state it felt a certain way to them—*like this,* as she might say after leaving the room.

TOLLENS: I'm with you so far. But what's the argument?

PONENS: In its simplest version, it's just this: Before Mary leaves the room, she knows all the physical information. When she leaves, she learns something new. So, the physical information isn't *all* the information: Physicalism is false. That's known as *the knowledge argument.*

TOLLENS: That last step . . .

PONENS: I said that was the simple version. Jackson gives a slightly more complete version in the article I quoted from a few minutes ago:

1. Mary (before her release) knows everything physical there is to know about other people.
2. Mary (before her release) does not know everything there is to know about other people (because she *learns* something about them on her release).

   Therefore,

3. There are truths about other people (and herself) which escape the physicalist story.

TOLLENS: Hmmm. That's worth thinking about.

BELLA: I don't know. I'm not sure I even agree with the first step.

TOLLENS: That step seems pretty good to me. Just think about it from Mary's perspective, before she leaves the room. She's wondering about the visual experiences of people outside who are looking at red roses. To her, what it's like to have such experiences is a mystery. For all she knows, those experiences might have the phenomenal quality that's produced by looking at green tree frogs.

PONENS: Well, she does know that there's a phenomenal difference between seeing green tree frogs and seeing red roses. But you're right: For all she knows, the phenomenal properties of such experiences could be the reverse of what they actually are. Come to think of it, you've basically stumbled on a third anti-physicalist argument—one that's distinct from Nagel's argument *and* the knowledge argument.

TOLLENS: That's me. I'm a stumbler.

PONENS: And some of your stumbles are inspired! Imagine a world just like ours in all physical respects. Each of us has a counterpart—a perfect duplicate in all physical and *almost* all mental respects. There's only one difference: Our counterparts are systematically inverted with respect to experiencing red and experiencing green. When you see a red rose, your inverted twin has a visual experience that's just like yours except for the color part. His experience is phenomenally similar to one you'd have if you were looking at a *green* rose. If you could see through his mind's eye, you'd be tempted to say, "Hey, that rose is green!" Seeing red roses causes him to have phenomenally green sensations, and seeing green frogs causes him to have phenomenally red sensations.

TOLLENS: So red and green are inverted.

PONENS: Right, but not the objective surface qualities of the frogs and the roses. Those are the same; you and your twin interact with exactly similar frogs and roses. Only the subjective effects of seeing those qualities are inverted. This is known as an "inverted spectrum" case.

BELLA: If that happened our counterparts wouldn't act anything like us! They'd think that stoplights were green!

TOLLENS: Not so fast, Sarah. Think about how we learned to use the word "red." Our twins' parents would have pointed at stop signs and fire trucks and said, "That color is red," just as our parents did. So, despite the inversion, our twins would say that things the color of stop signs, fire trucks, and the like are red. They'd stop at stoplights and go when the light turns green. They'd *behave* just as we do.

PONENS: That's right. The point is that we can conceive of a world in which the physical facts, including the behavioral facts, are just as they are while the phenomenal facts differ. Based on this idea, anti-physicalists have developed a new generation of conceivability arguments, similar to the argument we discussed last night, from Descartes.

BELLA: Gosh, I so regret missing *that* discussion.

PONENS: Actually, it was interesting. Descartes said . . .

BELLA: I think I'll pass on the history lesson. But as long as you're attacking science, we might as well hear all of your arguments at once. What are these so-called conceivability arguments?

PONENS: I'm not attacking science. Some of my best friends are scientists. Still, the Mary case and the inverted spectrum case do suggest that science has limits. The cases make it plausible that the complete physical truth fails to determine the nature of consciousness—what it's like to see red, for example. A third thought experiment indicates that the physical truth doesn't entail that consciousness even exists. Imagine a world of zombies.

TOLLENS: Whoa, that's a jump! Suddenly we're talking *Night of the Living Dead*?

PONENS: No, not flesh-eating zombies. The zombies I have in mind act exactly as we do. They're physically and functionally identical to ordinary human beings. But they lack consciousness: They have no conscious experience whatsoever. There's nothing it's like to be a zombie. It's all dark inside, so to speak.

BELLA: Pshaw!

TOLLENS: Did you just say "pshaw"?

BELLA: Yes.

TOLLENS: I didn't know people actually said that.

BELLA: I said it because this zombie business is just a version of that sophomoric question, "How do we know that other people have minds? How do we know that when I kick people . . ."

TOLLENS: Ow!

BELLA: How do I know that they feel pain? I never feel their pain, so why should I think they feel anything, let alone that their pain resembles mine?

PONENS: Why do you think those questions are sophomoric? They're harder to answer than you might think. Anyway, the argument I have in mind is different. Let's agree that you can know others feel pain. After all, even dualists usually believe in laws connecting brain states and experiences. If I feel pain every time my brain enters a certain state, I have reason to believe that you also feel pain when your brain enters that same type of state. That's just the way the world is set up.

BELLA: Agreed. But then what's the point of the zombie example, other than to creep me out?

PONENS: The example is meant to show that the complete physical truth doesn't guarantee that pain or any other state of consciousness exists. Imagine God making a world physically identical to the actual world. The brains of our counterparts are physically the same as ours: molecule-for-molecule. But their brain processes don't give rise to experience. That's just the way God sets things up.

TOLLENS: Wait. Their brains are *exactly* like ours physically? And yet they're zombies?

PONENS: Yes. I see nothing incoherent in that scenario. But if you don't buy the zombie case, there's always the inverted spectrum case. And if you don't buy either, just imagine God creating a world just like ours except for one small thing: Everybody's visual sensations are *slightly brighter* than ours. The physical facts are the same. It's just that everything looks a smidgen brighter, visually. That possibility doesn't seem to be excluded by the physical features of our brains. The synaptic connections, the chemical constitution of the neurons, and so on: All such physical features seem perfectly compatible with visual sensations that feel slightly brighter than ours do.

BELLA: I'm not so sure. Sounds speculative.

PONENS: Maybe, but there's a strong intuition here. The general point of all these examples is the same. The physical sciences tell us about the physical makeup of the brain. They also tell us what our brain states do—how they interact with each other, how they are caused, and how they engender behavior. But knowing such physical information doesn't justify drawing any definite inferences about experience. And if that's right, then it's hard to see why the physical truth would entail that consciousness exists, let alone that our experiences have this or that character.

TOLLENS: Okay, I think I get it. So remind me again of how these speculations relate to the Mary case and the knowledge argument.

PONENS: Again, the idea is that Mary can't figure out what it's like to see in color by drawing inferences from what she learns prerelease—even though there's not a single physical truth she doesn't know and even though she's a brilliant logician, unlimited in her inferential ability. Everything changes when she leaves the room and sees red. At that point, she can rule out possibilities that she couldn't rule out before leaving the room: She knows that seeing red feels *like this*, where "like this" refers to phenomenal redness as opposed to phenomenal greenness or phenomenal blueness. Her knowledge grows. And the conceivability argument—such as the argument involving zombies or the one involving inverted color experiences—is another spin on this. We can conceive of scenarios in which all of the physical facts are just as they actually are but consciousness doesn't exist or differs phenomenally from how it actually is. Those scenarios seem perfectly coherent, even after careful reflection.

TOLLENS: Huh.

PONENS: Right, and then a question arises: *Why* can we conceive of such things? And why are so many possibilities open to Mary before she leaves the room? Here the reasoning takes a metaphysical turn. According to proponents of the conceivability and knowledge arguments, the explanation is straightforward. The reason we can conceive of zombie scenarios and the like is that we recognize a basic truth: The physical facts don't metaphysically necessitate the facts about consciousness. That's also why so many possibilities are open to Mary before she leaves the room, despite her comprehensive physical knowledge. If this explanation is right, then the physical nature of the world isn't its complete nature. Physicalism is false.

TOLLENS: Huh.

BELLA: Well, boys, I remain unconvinced. But I'm too tired to do anything about it. I have a lot of work to do tomorrow, so I have to sleep.

TOLLENS: Yeah, I'm fading too. Can we continue this tomorrow night?

BELLA: This isn't as nice as the science library, but I could probably bear being here another night. I'll just sleep near the math books.

PONENS: Alright then. Until tomorrow.

Sarah Bella rolls off on her stool and disappears between two distant aisles. Ponens and Tollens put their arms over their faces and are soon snoring.

Wednesday Night

Scene: In the dark corner of the philosophy section, we find Ponens and Tollens, freshly shaven and to all appearances clean, along with the redoubtable Sarah Bella, who joins them once again on her rolling stool.

TOLLENS: Well, here we are again. Another night, another argument.

BELLA: I've been thinking about your arguments, Ponens, and I believe I know what's wrong with them.

PONENS: Alright, shoot.

TOLLENS: Hold on, hold on. I need a recap.

PONENS: Okay, first of all, the arguments each have two main steps. The first asserts that there's a disconnect between physical knowledge and phenomenal knowledge. In the knowledge argument, the disconnect is brought out by the Mary case—by the idea that, despite knowing all physical truths while still in the room, when she leaves she learns new truths about what it's like to see in color. In the conceivability argument, the disconnect is brought out by the zombie case, the inverted-spectrum case, and similar thought experiments—cases in which the physical truths are kept constant and the phenomenal truths are varied.

TOLLENS: So the first step concerns how we *know* or *conceive* of the physical and the phenomenal. There's not yet any conclusion about the relationship between the physical and the phenomenal themselves, right?

I mean, the arguments don't yet say that zombies are metaphysically possible or that physicalism is false?

PONENS: Right. The first step is sometimes called the "epistemic premise" because it concerns what is or can be known or conceived. And the disconnect that the premise asserts is sometimes called the "epistemic gap." The basic idea is that physical information alone can't tell us certain things about consciousness.

TOLLENS: Okay, got it. So the next step is . . .

PONENS: The metaphysical step. It's the part of the argument that asserts something about the nature of the world, rather than something about knowledge or understanding. In the case of the knowledge argument, the second step says that if what it's like to see in color can't be deduced from the physical truth then the physical truth doesn't necessitate the truth about what it's like to see in color. In the case of the conceivability argument, the second step takes the form of arguing that if zombies are conceivable then they are metaphysically possible. And if both steps are correct, then physicalism is false.

TOLLENS: Why?

PONENS: Physicalism must say, at the very least, that all truths about consciousness are metaphysically necessitated by physical truths. Otherwise, there would be truths about consciousness that go beyond the physical. And the anti-physicalist arguments purport to show that the world fails to satisfy this minimal condition for physicalism's truth: the metaphysical necessitation of the phenomenal by the physical.

TOLLENS: Well, I still have some questions. I think it might help to write out the arguments a little more explicitly.

PONENS: Okay, give me a minute.

Tollens disappears into the stacks. Forty-five minutes later, he returns to find Ponens writing feverishly, a pile of crumpled sheets of paper at his feet.

TOLLENS: Are you *still* not done?

PONENS: Good timing! I just finished. I wrote out three versions. One expresses the general structure of the arguments and the others summarize two specific versions:

The structure of the anti-physicalist arguments

Step 1 (Assert epistemic gap): There is an epistemic gap between the physical and the phenomenal.

Step 2 (Infer metaphysical gap): If there is an epistemic gap between the physical and the phenomenal, then there is a corresponding metaphysical gap, and so physicalism is false.

Conclusion: There is a metaphysical gap between the physical and the phenomenal, and so physicalism is false.

The knowledge argument

1. There are truths that are not deducible from the physical truth, namely, those Mary learns when she leaves the black-and-white room.
2. If there are truths that are not deducible from the physical truth, then there are truths that the physical truth does not necessitate, and so physicalism is false.
3. Therefore, there are truths that the physical truth does not necessitate, and so physicalism is false.

The conceivability argument (zombie version)

1. It is conceivable that there be zombies.
2. If it is conceivable that there be zombies, then it is metaphysically possible that there be zombies, and so physicalism is false.
3. Therefore, it is metaphysically possible that there be zombies, and so physicalism is false.

TOLLENS: Well, I'll give you this: Those arguments look reasonably straightforward.

PONENS: Thanks. I based these formulations on some work by Chalmers.

TOLLENS: Who?

PONENS: David Chalmers. He's probably done more than anyone else to sharpen and defend the anti-physicalist arguments. But I decided to simplify each step.

TOLLENS: Why?

PONENS: Because fully precise versions would be a bit complicated. We can add refinement if we need to.

TOLLENS: Fine with me. These versions make it easy to identify where I'm going to disagree anyway.

BELLA: Me too.

PONENS: Good. Where?

TOLLENS: These arguments have the same basic problem as Descartes' argument for dualism.

BELLA: Descartes again? That nonsense about the two realms?

TOLLENS: Exactly. Descartes believes he can infer possibility from clear and distinct conceivability. That idea didn't hold up too well on reflection, as even Ponens concedes. Right, Ponens?

PONENS: Right.

TOLLENS: Well, the arguments Ponens just summarized have a similar problem: They move illegitimately from a premise about what we know or can conceive to a conclusion about the world itself. It's the metaphysical inference—step 2—that I want to challenge.

PONENS: That's probably the most popular response to these arguments. So what's wrong with the inference, Tollens?

BELLA: Hold on there! I've done a little thinking about this too, and I say Tollens is conceding too much. The first, epistemic premise is false.

PONENS: Of which argument?

BELLA: It doesn't really matter, but I think the business about Mary makes the strongest case for the so-called epistemic gap, so I'll talk about the knowledge argument.

PONENS: That's fine. I doubt we'll miss much by focusing more on Mary than on zombies.

TOLLENS: Good. It's less creepy that way.

BELLA: Alright. I think Mary *could* figure out what it's like to see red even while sequestered in her black-and-white chamber.

PONENS: How?

BELLA: This came to me last night when I was trying to sleep. I had to squinch my eyes shut tightly because it's too bright in this library for me.

TOLLENS: It's too bright in here?

BELLA: I'm terribly sensitive to light. Anyway, so I was squinching my eyes, and I covered them with my hands. When I did that, I realized that when you push on your eyelid you see red! You can see a bit of an afterimage of redness just because of the pressure on your eye. Mary could do that. If she did, she'd learn what it's like to see red without going outside!

TOLLENS: Aw, that's just cheating. You could switch the example to a sort of experience you can't generate in that way.

BELLA: You're forgetting that Mary's super-smart and knows *all* the physical facts. She could probably figure out a way to get herself to have virtually *any* experience without leaving the room.

PONENS: Maybe, but that would be cheating pretty flagrantly, Sarah.

BELLA: How? It answers the argument, doesn't it?

PONENS: Not really. It's kinda like saying that Mary could get all the information from within the room by developing the ability to see through the walls. The claim is that she can't learn about what it's like to see red by drawing inferences from the objective, physical facts. You can't refute that claim by arranging for her to experience red firsthand without leaving the room. It doesn't matter how this experience is produced—by seeing red objects, by pressing on her eyes, by direct brain stimulation, or whatever. The point of keeping her in the room is to make it plausible that, at the first stage of the thought experiment, the only information she acquires about *color* experience is objective information of the sort provided by physics, chemistry, and so on, plus whatever she can deduce from that information. So, anything that allows her to have color experience while still in the room is, for all intents and purposes, equivalent to letting her go outside.

BELLA: That may be, but I can't help but think that the feeling that Mary learns something is just a result of our ignorance about what's involved in knowing all physical facts.

TOLLENS: I see. Ponens, I think Sarah's making a good point. It's hard to put yourself in Mary's shoes. Her physical knowledge seems daunting.

BELLA: Especially since physics and neuroscience are far from complete. I just don't buy the idea that Mary will have an impressive epiphany when she leaves the black-and-white room—not if she already knew everything in *completed* physics, chemistry, and neuroscience. Maybe a current textbook on the science of color vision won't teach her much about what it's like to see red. But if she learns the *completed* science, which fully explains how the human brain processes information acquired through visual perception, she'll be able to cause herself to have an experience that feels just like seeing a red tomato without leaving the room. To accomplish that feat, she might need some technology, such as brain-imaging machines. But the machines needn't have colored buttons or anything. If you think she learns something new when she leaves the room, you're probably just underestimating what her vast knowledge would enable her to accomplish without leaving.

PONENS: I don't think I'm making that mistake. I say only that Mary can't *deduce* what it's like to see red from objective physical information. I agree with what you say about what her vast knowledge would enable her to do. Again, maybe she could even come up with a way to see through walls and thereby perceive red things on the outside. But nothing of the kind pertains to what she can and can't deduce.

BELLA: Deduction, schmeduction! You philosophers care too much about that. Instead of taking logic classes, you should spend some time in a chemistry lab. If Mary can come to know what it's like to see red from within her room by using her scientific knowledge, then the physical information is in no way deficient.

PONENS: I'm not relying on deduction because of some fetish. Deduction is crucial because of its relation to necessity. If physicalism is true, then the physical truth is the whole truth. The physical truth should in that case leave nothing undetermined: It should necessitate all the truths, including the truths about consciousness.

TOLLENS: Agreed.

PONENS: So, the way the knowledge argument works is to show that the physical truth doesn't necessitate some phenomenal truths, namely, those concerning what it's like to see in color. To establish that failure of necessitation, the argument relies crucially on a claim that concerns deduction, namely, the claim that the phenomenal can't be deduced from the physical.

TOLLENS: Explain, please.

PONENS: If you'll allow me to sound algebraic for a moment—if you can deduce fact q from fact p, then you can see how p necessitates q.

TOLLENS: Okay. And?

PONENS: And coming to know q from p by means other than deduction offers no such guarantees. Suppose God wired my brain in such a way that after I memorized a thousand phone numbers from the Manhattan directory, I suddenly knew all of physics. That wouldn't show any deep connection between the nature of my Aunt June's phone number and the law of gravity.

BELLA: I wasn't suggesting anything that crazy.

PONENS: No, but that's the whole point of the Mary story. Since she can't deduce the truth about what it's like to see in color from the complete physical truth, there's reason to doubt that the complete physical truth metaphysically necessitates that phenomenal truth. And as we were saying last night, physicalism requires metaphysical necessitation of the phenomenal by the physical.

TOLLENS: So there's a lot of emphasis on deducibility here.

PONENS: You bet.

BELLA: Hold on! Last night when you were explaining that the Mary puzzle isn't just another version of the problem of other minds, you said that dualists can accept laws connecting consciousness to brain processes—laws of the form, "When someone has brain state X, she has phenomenal state Y." That was the idea, right?

PONENS: Right. So?

BELLA: Well, if Mary knows all the science, then she knows all the natural laws. So, she knows the laws that connect brain states with experiences. In particular, she knows laws connecting certain brain states with color experiences. Therefore, she can deduce what it's like to see red from those laws plus a full description of the brain states. So, by the very assumptions of the case, it follows that Mary *can* deduce what it's like to see red without leaving the room!

TOLLENS: No, that's wrong. Mary doesn't know *those* laws.

BELLA: Why not?!

TOLLENS: Because they're not purely *physical* laws. The black-and-white science lectures teach her all the physical laws, but no other laws. You said it yourself: The laws you're talking about have the form, "When someone has brain state X, she has phenomenal state Y."

BELLA: Okay, what's the problem with laws of that form?

TOLLENS: The X part is just a physical description, so that's fine. But the Y part will make use of phenomenal language, such as "what it's like."

PONENS: Exactly. These laws are sometimes called "bridge-laws" or, more specifically, "psycho-physical" laws, to highlight the fact that they connect distinct domains. They contrast with physical laws, which concern only the physical domain.

BELLA: So you're saying that Mary can't know these laws even though they're about brain states? Why isn't that just loading the dice against her? Who's cheating now?

PONENS: Again, prerelease Mary knows all the *physical* laws. If all truths are physical, then that should be enough. If there are further, psycho-physical laws that she doesn't know and can't figure out, then that just goes to show that knowing what it's like to see in color requires more than just knowing physical information—which is the point of the thought experiment.

TOLLENS: That makes me wonder: Shouldn't we say that Mary does know everything before she leaves the room, but she just hasn't been hooked up to certain parts of the physical world in the right way?

PONENS: Hooked up?

TOLLENS: Right. She knows everything about the human visual system. She seems to learn something when she leaves the room only because her own visual system hasn't been activated in such a way as to produce color experience.

PONENS: Is this an objection to the first premise, the epistemic premise that says she learns something once she leaves the room? Or is it an objection to the second premise, the inference to the metaphysical gap?

TOLLENS: Hmmm. I'm not sure. You're the logician.

PONENS: Well, does she learn something once she leaves the room or doesn't she?

TOLLENS: No, she just becomes hooked up to a process she already knew about.

PONENS: Yeah, but in doing so, doesn't she learn about experiences? Doesn't she learn something that she didn't know about other people's experiences, namely, what it's like to have such experiences?

TOLLENS: Okay, I guess so.

PONENS: So you're denying premise 2?

TOLLENS: Actually, right now I think I'm denying premise 1. According to that premise, when Mary leaves the room she learns something even though she already knew all the physical facts. Perhaps, though, what she learns is physical. Maybe you just can't know all the physical facts without being hooked up to the world in a certain way. Maybe the mistake is the assumption that all the physical facts are deducible from what Mary can learn in the room. Is it so surprising that knowing some of the physical facts requires that Mary actually get out and *have* some experiences?

BELLA: I think you might have something there.

PONENS: That sounds pretty good at first, but on reflection I think it's giving up the game.

TOLLENS: How's that?

PONENS: Think about what makes an item of information *physical.* Whatever else physical information is, it must be the sort of information science reveals—or at least it must be metaphysically necessitated by the sort of information science reveals. And that seems to imply that all physical information is objective.

TOLLENS: Objective?

PONENS: Yes. If a fact is physical, you shouldn't have to have any particular sort of sensory capacity to understand it. Intelligent aliens, who have very different sorts of conscious experiences, should be able to understand any scientific theory, just as they should be able to understand any mathematical proof. It should—at least in principle—be possible to translate the theory into a language they can understand, without losing information.

TOLLENS: Hmmm. I need to think about that. Something seems fishy.

BELLA: No, I agree with Ponens on this. Science is all about the ability to verify things intersubjectively. This is one thing that Nagel guy got right. If bat consciousness is physical, we should be able to learn everything about bats without experiencing the world in the way they do. If we give up on that project, we sacrifice one of the main ideals of science.

PONENS: Exactly.

BELLA: But I think something of Tollens' point is still salvageable, and it has to do with your insistence on deduction. Maybe there's a simple explanation for why Mary can't deduce what it's like to see red from the physical truth: The physical truth is taught to her in scientific language, and she wasn't given a translation manual.

TOLLENS: What?

BELLA: The proposition that *some* room is small follows logically from the proposition that *this* room is small. True?

TOLLENS: True.

BELLA: But suppose you don't know German. Then you can't infer "Some room is small" just from "Dieses Zimmer ist klein," which is German for "This room is small." The conclusion follows logically from the fact expressed by that German sentence. But since you don't know German, you can't deduce that conclusion from what you are told. So, no wonder Mary can't deduce information formulated in the language of experience from information formulated in the language of physics. That's not a limitation of physics or on what truths can be deduced from the physical truth. It's a just a point about translation and language.

TOLLENS: Woohoo! Look who's the logician now!

BELLA: I never said I didn't take logic. I just didn't get obsessed with it.

PONENS: Your point about deduction sounds right, Sarah. But it doesn't imply what you think it does. We're assuming Mary knows all the physical facts about color vision before she leaves the room. We can also assume she knows all other physical facts, and that presumably includes the linguistic facts. So she understands all human languages and can do all the translations needed to perform the relevant deductions.

BELLA: Look, I was using the example of German only as sort of a metaphor. The language of experience is distinctive and presents unique translation problems. To acquire the concepts involved in comprehending that language, you need to have certain experiences—or at least stand in some close relationship to such experiences.

PONENS: Ah, so this point is more about *concepts* than *words*.

BELLA: Right. The idea is that Mary could deduce the facts about experience from the physical facts—if only she had the relevant phenomenal concepts. By keeping her hostage in her room, you're preventing her from having those concepts. So, the premise that she learns something when she leaves the room doesn't show that the phenomenal facts can't be deduced from the physical facts. At most, the premise shows that doing the deduction requires having, or standing in an appropriate relation to, certain sorts of experience.

PONENS: Okay, I think I get it.

TOLLENS: I don't.

PONENS: You don't really need to, Tollens: This response has the same problem that the hooked-up response has. If Mary learns something substantial by exiting her room and seeing a rose, then there's information that can't be understood independently of one's experiences and sensory capacities. And that violates the objectivity condition on physical information.

TOLLENS: That was the idea that understanding physical information never requires adopting a particular type of viewpoint or having a specific type of experience, right?

PONENS: Right. The contrast with German is telling, in two ways. First, languages like German could be learned by Mary while still in the room. The fact that she can't learn "the language of experience" in the same way casts doubt on the analogy between these two "languages." Second, if you knew that this room was small, "learning" the truth of the German sentence wouldn't teach you anything new. You might be confused when someone says, "Dieses Zimmer ist klein." But when it was translated for you, you would say, "Ah, that's just German for 'This room is small.'" Since you already knew that this room was small, learning that the German sentence is true wouldn't be learning a new fact about rooms. You wouldn't have a revelation of the sort Mary has when she sees red, except maybe a revelation about translation or language.

TOLLENS: So the German for "room" is "Zimmer"?

PONENS: That's all you took away from what I just said?

TOLLENS: Well, I'm still not sure I get it.

PONENS: I think I can make more or less the same point in another way. After Mary leaves the room, she acquires the concepts needed to do the relevant deductions, right?

TOLLENS: Seems so.

PONENS: Now she knows all the physical facts *and* all the phenomenal facts about color vision. Even so, she wasn't able to deduce those phenomenal facts from the physical facts *alone*. And she *still* can't do that deduction, even after she knows that which is to be deduced—not from only the physical facts.

TOLLENS: Why not?

PONENS: Think of it this way. After leaving the room, she knows all the physical facts *and* she knows what it's like to see red. Even so, she could conceive of the following scenario: The physical facts are exactly the same but consciousness doesn't exist; our bodies—including our brains—are just as they actually are but no one experiences anything. She knows that's not how the world actually is, but she can coherently imagine such a world. If she could *deduce* the experiential facts from the physical facts, such a scenario would seem incoherent to her.

TOLLENS: Ah, I see. So this is sort of *The Revenge of the Zombies*!

PONENS: If you want to put it that way, yes.

TOLLENS: "Brains, I want brains . . ."

BELLA: We all want what we lack.

TOLLENS: That's cold.

BELLA: Speaking of cold, don't you find it hot in here?

PONENS: Actually, I'm freezing.

TOLLENS: Oh, no. Not this again.

BELLA: I'm going to give this one last try; then I'm going to sleep.

TOLLENS: Like a pit bull, this one!

BELLA: Persistence is a virtue.

TOLLENS: So is silence. You're one of those students that just dominates class discussions, aren't you?

BELLA: I'm not going to dignify that with a response. So it strikes me that maybe the best strategy isn't to deny that Mary learns anything. In a sense, she does.

PONENS: Finally, a concession!

BELLA: Hold on. She gains knowledge in a way, but not the way we've been assuming. We've been assuming that what she learns are truths: facts, information, true propositions. Maybe that's the flaw in the argument. Perhaps she learns something when she leaves the room but not in the sense that she gains information. She doesn't learn that something is the case. Instead she learns *how to do* something. What she gains is know-how. She gains abilities, not information.

TOLLENS: Abilities? What abilities?

BELLA: Imaginative abilities, for one thing. She learns how to imagine seeing red, that is, how to visualize that color. She also gains the ability to distinguish red things from blue things by sight. That's why it's so hard to articulate what she learns without resorting to flaky terminology such as "what it's like" or "red looks like *that*." It's because *what she learns* isn't a fact at all.

TOLLENS: Huh. Interesting. But why does it matter if we describe what she learns as an ability instead of a fact?

BELLA: It changes everything. If her increase in knowledge consists in the acquisition of abilities, then physicalism is off the hook. Physicalism says that all truths about consciousness are physical; it does *not* say that science lessons can teach you how to imagine in this way or that. The Mary case shows something about imagination and other abilities. It doesn't establish the existence of nonphysical, phenomenal information. There is no such thing.

TOLLENS: I see. So this is a sort of "have your cake and eat it too" view. You grant that Mary learns all physical information through watching the black-and-white lectures *and* that she gains knowledge when she leaves the room and sees red. But since her epistemic growth involves gaining abilities instead of information, the case provides no reason to doubt that all information is physical. Neat.

BELLA: Thank you.

PONENS: I agree, this strategy is elegant. It's really an instance of a more general strategy: Accept the claim that Mary gains knowledge, but argue that her new knowledge is of type X, where X is not informational knowledge. Other instances of this general strategy could be developed.

TOLLENS: Such as?

PONENS: The most obvious one is where type X is acquaintance knowledge—knowing a thing, as when you know a city or a person, rather than knowing that such-and-such is the case. One might say that Mary's knowledge gain consists in becoming acquainted with a property, in the way that you can become acquainted with a person you've previously only read about.

BELLA: You're digressing. I didn't say anything about acquaintance knowledge.

PONENS: Sorry. Well anyway, as I was saying, your strategy is elegant, Sarah.

BELLA: Thanks for the compliment, but that sounded a bit backhanded.

PONENS: I guess it was. I don't think these strategies work, in the end. You may be right that Mary gains some abilities when she leaves the room. But that doesn't mean she doesn't *also* gain information.

BELLA: True, but why add that? The assumption that she gains abilities explains her epistemic growth, as Tollens put it. If that's right, then I see no reason to say that she gains information as well.

TOLLENS: Wait, you're saying that Mary gains new abilities but doesn't learn anything new about the world? Doesn't it seem that she gains those abilities precisely *because* she gains information?

BELLA: I don't see why I'm forced to say that.

TOLLENS: Well, think about the ability to, say, sort fish—to distinguish fresh fish from older fish in the grocery store.

PONENS: Don't tell me you know how to do that.

TOLLENS: I had an uncle who was a fishmonger.

PONENS: May wonders never cease.

TOLLENS: So, among other things, I can sort the fish because I know that the eyes of fresh fish are less cloudy than those of their more questionable cousins. I know a certain fact about fish eyes. That's what gives me the relevant ability.

BELLA: Okay, I get it. But why think all cases work that way?

TOLLENS: I'm not saying they do. What's a good example of someone gaining an ability without gaining information?

BELLA: Here's one. Before I started taking yoga, I couldn't touch my toes. After stretching for a while, I could. Did I learn some new truth? I don't think so.

PONENS: But did you *learn* something in anything like the sense that Mary does when she leaves the room? You didn't have any revelation when your fingers and toes first met, did you? No epiphany?

BELLA: Well, it did feel pretty good. But no, I guess not.

PONENS: But Mary *does* have an epiphany when she first sees in color. You conceded that, right?

BELLA: I did, for the sake of argument. Anyway, all you've shown is that the analogy isn't perfect. It might still be good enough: When Mary leaves the room she gains only know-how, just as I gained only know-how when I learned to touch my toes.

TOLLENS: I don't know, Bella. I liked your idea when I first heard it, but it's starting to sound bad. I mean, didn't you already know how to touch your toes before you were able to do so? Isn't that why you stretched the particular muscles that you did?

BELLA: I wasn't completely in the dark, but I still learned something.

TOLLENS: "Stretching as learning." I love it!

PONENS: I don't know. To my nose, this analysis of Mary's learning in terms of gaining abilities smells fishy.

BELLA: Tell me what's wrong with it, then.

PONENS: I think it's possible to learn what it's like without gaining the sorts of abilities you mentioned.

BELLA: How could that happen?

PONENS: Here's one possibility. When Mary leaves the room, she sees a red rose. Let's say the specific shade is vermilion. Now, to my eyes, vermilion is almost indistinguishable from cadmium red.

TOLLENS: Ah, to my eyes too. It's always a problem.

PONENS: So, suppose we take away her vermilion rose, so that she no longer can see it.

BELLA: That's cruel. You'd take away her first red rose?

PONENS: There's purpose in my cruelty. So we take away the rose. Arguably, she still knows what it's like to see that specific shade of red: vermilion. At least, she retains that knowledge for a little while after the rose disappears. Even so, she might not be able to imagine and reidentify that exact shade of red. When asked to imagine seeing vermilion, we can suppose, it's as likely that she would wind up imagining cadmium red. Also, she can't reliably distinguish a vermilion color swatch from a cadmium-red swatch. So, knowing what it's like to see vermilion shouldn't be identified with being able to imagine or identify that specific shade.

TOLLENS: Nice. I think your point holds for related abilities as well, such as the ability to remember a specific shade. We can't identify knowing what it's like with any such abilities, either individually or in combination, since you can have the knowledge without the associated abilities. Q.E.D.!

PONENS: Well said, Tollens. And I can think of another way to separate what Mary learns from the abilities that she acquires when she leaves the room. When the door to the outside finally opens, she's excited. She leaps from her chair and runs as fast as she can. But on the way out, she bumps her head.

TOLLENS: Ah, Mary! Brilliant but clumsy!

PONENS: It's not unprecedented: Remember Thales and the well. Anyway, the accident causes brain damage, and as a result her imaginative capacities become severely limited. Then she sees the rose. She stares at it and takes in the redness. She has the expected revelation about what it's like. But she can't imagine anything to save her life! She knows what it's like to see red while staring at the rose, but the moment she turns away she can't imagine seeing red. So, while staring at the rose, she has phenomenal knowledge—she knows what it's like to see red—without the corresponding imaginative ability. And the same reasoning applies to sorting abilities.

BELLA: You guys have conversations like this a lot, don't you?

TOLLENS: You can tell?

BELLA: You're pretty good at coming up with clever little examples.

TOLLENS: Did I hear you give us a compliment? Color me amazed!

BELLA: I mean you guys may be too clever—or too imaginative—for your own good. Regarding your first example, about the specific shades of red, why assume that Mary knows what it's like to see vermilion if she's unable to reliably reidentify that shade? She may know what it's like to see shades that fall within a certain range, but does she know what it's like to see vermilion in particular? I see no reason to think so.

TOLLENS: I guess we haven't proven that part of the argument.

BELLA: And your second example, about Mary's bumping her head and losing her ability to visualize—that one isn't much better. It relies on dubious assumptions about how the brain works. In the human brain, perception and imagination are closely linked. If Mary's brain is damaged in the way you suppose, it's unlikely that she'd know much of anything about seeing red. With respect to that knowledge, she's not much more than a vegetable.

TOLLENS: Poor Mary. First a captive, then a cucumber.

PONENS: Sarah, I'm not sure you're right about how close perception and imagination are linked in normal human brains. But suppose you are. Even so, we can imagine a Mary-type character whose brain works differently. In her brain, the faculties of imagination and perception are separable. One could lose one ability without losing the other. If your analysis of Mary's knowledge gain is correct, then it should apply to this other character too. The knowledge argument doesn't depend on Mary's being a typical human being. She's atypical anyway. No actual person reasons as well as she does.

TOLLENS: I think he's got you there, Sarah.

PONENS: Also, I find your analysis of the Mary case questionable. She might gain abilities when she leaves the room, but is that really all she gains? That seems implausible. If anything, she gains abilities because, not instead, of her acquisition of phenomenal information—as Tollens said earlier. But if you stick to your guns, I'm not sure I can do much to stop you.

BELLA: I certainly don't see anything contradictory in my view.

PONENS: The theories maintaining that the Earth is flat and that the sun revolves around the Earth aren't self-contradictory either. I don't see you jumping for those theories!

BELLA: That's unfair. There's empirical evidence against the flat-Earth and geocentric theories. You've mentioned no such evidence against my ability analysis. So, why is my analysis implausible? Because you guys don't buy it?

PONENS: Look, we've constructed two potential counterexamples. To block them, it's got to be plausible that Mary's acquiring the sorts of abilities you invoke accounts for the revelation she has when she finally sees red. Otherwise, the analysis doesn't explain the data.

BELLA: Data? What data?

PONENS: I mean the intuition that Mary gains knowledge when she leaves the room. I doubt her gain in knowledge can be plausibly explained as a gain in abilities—unless those abilities are accompanied by precisely the sort of phenomenal information that, according to you, doesn't exist.

BELLA: As I said: My theory seems implausible to you because you don't buy it.

TOLLENS: No, Sarah, that's not right. Your view faces a dilemma. When Mary leaves the room, she gains either *abilities but no information* or *abilities plus information.* If she gains abilities but no information, then what happens to her doesn't look much like an increase in *knowledge* at all, as when you acquired the ability to touch your toes. This would make it unclear why she would have a revelation.

PONENS: Exactly.

TOLLENS: And if she gains not only abilities but information too, as the other horn of the dilemma says, then we're back where we started. The Mary case seems to show that there's phenomenal information that can't be deduced from physical information. The idea that she gains abilities *also*, and that this *partly* explains her postrelease epistemic growth, is neither here nor there. There's still that new information to reckon with.

PONENS: Yes. And I think a similar dilemma will arise for the acquaintance-knowledge version of Sarah's strategy. Maybe Mary gains acquaintance knowledge when she leaves the room. But if you try to say that that's *all* she gains, the explanation of her revelation starts looking implausible. And if you accept that she *also* gains information, then you've done nothing to block the epistemic premise of the knowledge argument. I think this problem will arise for *any* version of the "Mary gains noninformational knowledge of type X" strategy.

BELLA: I think we may be at a standoff. I doubt we'll get much further tonight. I will say this, though. Your criticisms boil down to the complaint that my theory is counterintuitive and surprising in various ways. And I'm willing to grant that. But so what? The truth is often counterintuitive and surprising, as more than three centuries of science have shown. And I'd rather go with a counterintuitive physicalist theory than one that says consciousness is a nonphysical phenomenon totally different from everything else. My view may not be intuitively plausible, but yours is positively spooky.

TOLLENS: I'm with you there, but I'd go about things a different way. I think . . .

BELLA: I think it's time to sleep. I'm verging on the brain damage you guys want to give to poor Mary.

PONENS: Alright. Back to the math aisles for you?

BELLA: Yeah, and back to the science library tomorrow night. This is getting frustrating.

TOLLENS: In a good way, I hope.

BELLA: Let's just say I'll probably be sleeping in the science library from now on.

PONENS: Alright then. 'Night Ms. Bella.

BELLA: 'Night boys. Don't let the book-bugs bite.

Sarah Bella wheels away toward the mathematics books. Ponens and Tollens begin constructing their makeshift pillows.

PONENS: Sleep well, Tollens.

TOLLENS: Wait one second, Ponens. It strikes me there may be another way to argue that Mary doesn't learn anything new when she leaves the room.

PONENS: Okay, but make it quick. I'm fading fast.

TOLLENS: Last night you mentioned that cognitive science has gone some way toward explaining thought.

PONENS: I did.

TOLLENS: I've actually read a bit about that. Apparently, a good deal is known about how the mind represents the world.

PONENS: You mean how thoughts and experiences can be about things?

TOLLENS: Right. For example, our current visual experiences represent books and library furniture.

PONENS: It's true, cognitive science has had a lot to say about mental representation. But we're not talking about representation. We're talking about consciousness.

TOLLENS: Well, you've been talking about the phenomenal properties of color vision. Isn't it a bit odd that cognitive science can explain how color vision represents, and physics can explain the nature of what it represents, but neither science can explain what it's like to represent?

PONENS: Perhaps it's odd, but it seems to be true nonetheless. That's what the Mary case shows.

TOLLENS: Yeah, but when you take a step back, it's pretty difficult to get a grasp on what these sciences are supposed to be missing.

PONENS: How so?

TOLLENS: Well, it's not as though when you look at a rose you notice two things, the red of the rose *and* the phenomenal redness of your experience. You just see the red of the rose. The experience is transparent, so to speak. It's as though you see right through it to the red of the rose.

PONENS: I don't know about that.

TOLLENS: It seems intuitive to me. And if experience is transparent, and if there's no difficulty explaining in physical terms either redness or how we represent redness, then it's hard to see what else needs explaining.

PONENS: But what about *what it's like* to see red?

TOLLENS: Perhaps that's just another way to talk about the nature of visual representation, which can be explained physically.

PONENS: I agree with part of what you're saying. Phenomenal properties are probably involved in mental representation. But the idea that they're *just* representational properties, with no remainder, seems doubtful. Still, some prominent philosophers have recently come to endorse that view. It's usually called "representationalism."

TOLLENS: Ah! I should have known I'd stumbled upon another "ism." So maybe I'm missing something, but why won't representationalism solve our problem?

PONENS: Assuming that theory is true?

TOLLENS: Yes.

PONENS: Okay. Suppose experience is transparent. And suppose phenomenal properties are just representational properties. Even so, phenomenal properties still represent in a distinctive, phenomenal way.

TOLLENS: What does that mean?

PONENS: You can represent a red tomato in all sorts of different ways: through vision, hearing, touch—maybe even unconsciously.

TOLLENS: Okay. So?

PONENS: Well, what about the distinctive way in which color vision represents—the phenomenal manner of representation? How is cognitive science supposed to explain that? We're just where we were before we brought representationalism onto the scene, only now Mary has to rephrase her questions in representational terms. She'll wonder, "What is it like to represent redness in the way that those outside do, when they see red roses?" Is that progress?

TOLLENS: I guess not.

PONENS: You guess right. Whether or not representationalism is true, it still seems clear that Mary gains information when she goes outside and sees a rose. It doesn't matter much if that information concerns *representational* features of experience rather than *non*representational features. Either way, the knowledge argument's epistemic premise goes through.

TOLLENS: Okay, that's all the fight I can give against the epistemic premise. Mary gains information. I admit it. Can we sleep now?

PONENS: Sleep away.

Thursday Night

Scene: Ponens and Tollens are walking through the stacks on tiptoes, peeking around corners. Ponens opens the door to the stairwell and looks around. He then walks back to their established corner near the philosophy section to find Tollens sitting on the rolling stool recently occupied by Sarah Bella.

PONENS: Where'd you find that?

TOLLENS: She left it next to the math books.

PONENS: You're just rolling around on that thing because she did.

TOLLENS: Whatever. She was onto something. It's fun to scoot. Anyway, did you find anyone?

PONENS: No. It looks like tonight we have the floor to ourselves.

TOLLENS: Good. I don't like finding out halfway through the night that we're not alone. It's creepy. Not zombie-creepy, but creepy nonetheless.

PONENS: Judging by your freshly shaven appearance yesterday, you didn't seem to find Sarah creepy.

TOLLENS: Hey, sometimes you don't know how dodgy you look until you see yourself through the eyes of another. And by the way, you radiated a sort of fresh scent yourself. I don't suppose that was accidental.

PONENS: Well, you know, you walk through the perfume section of the department store, and you can hardly avoid getting misted by something or other.

TOLLENS: Sure. That's always happening. All the time.

PONENS: Okay, okay, seriously, though, I was surprised that you took my side of the argument more often than not.

TOLLENS: Well, it's just hard to deny that Mary acquires information when she leaves the room. The example is a good one. And I just couldn't buy that stuff about abilities.

PONENS: So I've persuaded you? You've given up on physicalism?

TOLLENS: Not so fast. I said I think Mary acquires information—so I'm granting your epistemic premise. But I still think the knowledge argument fails. The problem is the second premise, the inference from the epistemic gap to the metaphysical gap.

PONENS: Ah. I thought you might have forgotten that step.

TOLLENS: Who do you think you're talking to? Today, while you were loitering in the perfume section of Macy's, I did some reading.

PONENS: There goes my edge.

TOLLENS: Exactly. It turns out several philosophers defend my position. As some put it, there's an *explanatory* gap between the physical and the phenomenal. Objective theories of the sort one finds in physics, chemistry, and so on really do come up short. They leave it mysterious why physical phenomena such as brain processes should be accompanied by conscious experience. The gap is deep. It may even be unbridgeable. That's what the Mary case, the zombie case, and the other thought experiments we've been discussing show.

PONENS: Right!

TOLLENS: Hold on, there. The result is significant, but the significance is epistemic, not metaphysical. The gap concerns how the physical-phenomenal relation can be explained, not what the relation consists in. So, even though there's an explanatory gap, there need be no metaphysical gap of the sort you dualists believe in. Consciousness could still be physical. And in my view, it is.

PONENS: That's a pretty attractive stance. But it's harder to defend than you might think.

TOLLENS: I don't see why. The basic strategy for resisting the knowledge argument was already in place when we discussed Descartes. Remember what we were saying about Clark Kent and Superman?

PONENS: Unfortunately.

TOLLENS: A similar move can be made here. Mary acquires information when she leaves the room, but only in a metaphysically innocuous sense. She learns something she already knew.

PONENS: I'm not following. Either she gains information or she doesn't. If she gains information, then she didn't have that information before. And since she had all the physical information before, her new information is nonphysical. That result doesn't sound metaphysically innocuous to me.

TOLLENS: Let me put it this way. Lois Lane and Clark Kent both work for a newspaper, *The Daily Globe.* Suppose they're on an assignment that requires them to be at the top of the Empire State Building. While up there, Clark notices that Lois is wearing kryptonite earrings. He takes a quick step back and, whoops, begins to fall off the building. Lois is standing there, looking over the edge in horror. Meanwhile, Clark, aka Superman, doesn't have time to change into his cape and stuff and has little choice but to start flying. Lois is astonished. She learns that Clark Kent can fly!

PONENS: Okay, so she learns a new fact, just as Mary does.

TOLLENS: Yeah, but in an important sense, she already knew what she supposedly just learned. She knew *of that guy*—the guy who is both Clark Kent and Superman—that he could fly. She just didn't know it under the Clark Kent disguise.

PONENS: So facts wear disguises, like superheroes?

TOLLENS: In a way. A single fact can be expressed in different ways. Consider the statements, "Superman can fly" and "Clark Kent can fly." Someone not in the know might believe only the first is true. But really, it can't be that *only* one of the two statements is true. If one is true, so is the other. That's because they represent the same fact—that a certain guy can fly. They represent that fact in different ways, but it's the same fact nonetheless.

PONENS: Well, there's room for disagreement about the semantics. But let's suppose you're right. Why does this matter here? The Mary case is about consciousness, not language.

TOLLENS: The point I wanted to make isn't just about language. Suppose Lois makes a potion that causes Superman to fall in love with her.

PONENS: I thought he was in love with her already.

TOLLENS: That's because of the potion!

PONENS: I don't think the stories specify whether his love resulted from Lois' natural charms or her way with chemical potions.

TOLLENS: Perhaps we should set that momentous scholarly issue aside.

PONENS: Oh, fine. But I'm right.

TOLLENS: Anyway, suppose Lois gives Superman the potion and it works. It follows that Clark Kent falls for her. She can't make Superman fall for her while Clark Kent remains indifferent. Not even God could do that. They're the same person! Clark Kent's loving her and Superman's loving her are one and the same.

PONENS: Okay, okay, I get it. But how is this supposed to apply to the Mary case?

TOLLENS: Take one thing that Mary learns when she leaves the room—say, what it's like to see red.

PONENS: Okay.

TOLLENS: She expresses this new knowledge when she leaves the room by saying, "Aha! Seeing red feel like *this!*"

PONENS: Suppose she does.

TOLLENS: That's just like Lois Lane seeing Clark Kent fly. Mary might think she's learning a new fact, but really she's just "learning" something she already knew in a different disguise. She already knew that when people see red their brains enter a certain state—one that her brain had never entered. When she walks out and sees a rose, though, and actually has that brain state, she comes to know the same fact in a new way. She expresses it differently, and she may be surprised. But that says more about the way she *knows* the fact than it does about the fact itself. To use a spatial metaphor, she comes to know from the inside the same fact that she already knew from the outside.

PONENS: I see. There's definitely something right in what you're saying.

TOLLENS: Thank you.

PONENS: You're welcome. But you're missing an important point.

TOLLENS: Which is?

PONENS: Mary is not Lois Lane.

TOLLENS: Yes, well, I wasn't confused about that part. I was using a little thing called an *analogy*.

PONENS: Yes, but the analogy doesn't hold: Unlike Lois, Mary is supposed to know everything physical before leaving the room. If everything is physical, as physicalism says, then Mary would know everything. The case of Lois Lane couldn't be more different. She doesn't even know that her colleague changes into spandex when he enters telephone booths! She doesn't know that those glasses he wears don't have corrective lenses! Compared to Mary, Lois is an ignoramus.

TOLLENS: You don't have to be rude about it. Lois is a hard-working woman. A damn fine reporter. What's the big deal?

PONENS: The big deal is that there are facts that she doesn't know under any disguise. It's Lois' ignorance of those facts that allows her to get confused about the identity of Superman and Clark Kent.

TOLLENS: So?

PONENS: So the analogy breaks down at a crucial juncture. On your view, when Mary leaves the room she merely comes to represent in new ways facts she already knows. There aren't any facts about seeing red that she didn't already know under some disguise before leaving the room.

TOLLENS: Correct.

PONENS: Well, that's totally different from what happens to Lois Lane. She knows Superman flies without knowing that fact under the Clark Kent disguise only because she doesn't know certain other facts. For example, she doesn't know that Clark Kent changes into Superman's clothes at opportune moments. If you gave her all such information, she'd be in a position to see through the disguise of all of the facts concerning Clark Kent and Superman. She'd be able to recognize that all such facts concern the same person. Unless she's a poor reasoner, she wouldn't be surprised to see Clark Kent fly.

TOLLENS: Fair enough. So?

PONENS: So, Lois' ignorance generates her confusion. This suggests a principle:

> *Disguise Depends on Ignorance.* In order to know a fact under one disguise but not under another, one must be ignorant of some distinct fact or make a mistake in reasoning.

TOLLENS: Okay, suppose that's right. What follows?

PONENS: Hear me out. According to Disguise Depends on Ignorance, if Mary just learns an old fact in a new disguise when she leaves the room then there are two possibilities: Either she's ignorant of some distinct fact or she's making a mistake in reasoning. She makes no such mistake; by hypothesis, she's a flawless logical reasoner. So, she must be ignorant of some distinct fact. But what could that fact be? If physicalism is true, then there aren't any facts that she doesn't know before leaving the room. She learns all the facts, including the phenomenal facts, while still in the room. She learns them under the physical disguise, so to speak.

TOLLENS: I get the sense you've thought about this before.

PONENS: I think my example was Zorro, but yes, you're right.

TOLLENS: Superman's better. I don't even know Zorro's real name.

PONENS: Don Diego de la Vega.

TOLLENS: Ahh. Right. Well, I agree with you that the Mary case may not be exactly like the Lois case. But that doesn't falsify my old-fact/new-disguise view. At most, you've shown that my view conflicts with Disguise Depends on Ignorance. Why should we believe that principle?

PONENS: Given what we said about Lois Lane and Superman, doesn't it seem obviously true?

TOLLENS: Obvious? You philosophers don't think it's obvious that your socks exist!

PONENS: Fair enough.

TOLLENS: Alright, so let me get clear again on what you take the argument to be. If all the facts are physical, then Mary should be able to deduce all facts about color experience from the facts she learns in the black-and-white room.

PONENS: Right.

TOLLENS: The idea seems to be that if there are two ways of knowing about something, whether it's Superman or the sensation of redness, enough knowledge about that thing will allow us to move by deductive reasoning from the one way of thinking about that thing to the other.

PONENS: Right.

TOLLENS: So what I'm wondering is why that has to be true across the board. Couldn't it be that our minds don't always work that way? Perhaps some of the ways we think about things involve cognitive states that we simply can't reason our way into. Put another way, perhaps in some cases we're prevented from reasoning from one concept or proposition to another by sort of a brute neural force. Maybe certain sorts of concepts are causally and cognitively isolated from one another.

PONENS: Hmmm. Well, I suppose that's possible. But that doesn't fit the Lois Lane case. And I see no reason why my analysis of that case, in terms of Disguise Depends on Ignorance, doesn't generalize.

TOLLENS: Probably it does, for the most part. But maybe the principle doesn't apply to the case at hand—physical concepts and phenomenal concepts.

PONENS: Isn't it suspicious that the principle should hold in every case *except* the one that creates a problem for physicalism? That seems a bit desperate, doesn't it?

TOLLENS: No, not if there are special reasons to expect an exception. And in this case, there are such reasons.

PONENS: I'm listening.

TOLLENS: Consider the different roles physical and phenomenal concepts play in our thinking. Physical concepts, including those developed in neuroscience, are theoretical concepts. We develop them in the course of theorizing to explain what we observe. Phenomenal concepts seem different. They're used in perceptual recognition. You recognize that something is yellow, say, because when you see it you have a characteristic visual experience. You recognize the experience as being *like that*. Phenomenal concepts figure into the *like that* part of your perceptual recognition.

PONENS: Go on.

TOLLENS: There are reasons to suspect that our perceptual and recognitional abilities evolved much earlier than our ability to reason abstractly. Before we can sit around and theorize, we had better be able to flee from predators, avoid poisonous berries, and detect foods to sustain us. All of these things would be facilitated by our evolving a way of perceiving that involves experience.

PONENS: Hmmm. Can you really do evolutionary neuroscience while sitting in an armchair?

TOLLENS: Armchair? This is a stool.

PONENS: Don't be difficult. You know what I mean.

TOLLENS: Okay, what I'm saying is speculative. I admit that. But isn't it *likely* that my evolutionary story, or something along similar lines, is true?

PONENS: I'm not sure. Anyway, you're suggesting only that these two ways of thinking about the world, experientially and theoretically, probably developed at different stages of evolution. Suppose that's right. It doesn't follow that once the two ways evolved they became cognitively isolated.

TOLLENS: Maybe not, but the evolutionary point is suggestive. If the two sorts of concepts evolved independently, then we shouldn't be surprised if they turn out to be cognitively isolated. And that possibility seems even more likely when we consider its survival advantages.

PONENS: More speculation?

TOLLENS: Sorry, the laboratories are locked. Here's the idea. Phenomenal concepts not only *refer* to phenomenal states and phenomenal properties. When you entertain thoughts involving phenomenal concepts, you tend to *have* experiences—experiences that phenomenally resemble those picked out by those concepts.

PONENS: Faint copies of the experiences?

TOLLENS: Right, faint copies.

PONENS: Yeah, Hume said something similar. I'm not sure about this view of phenomenal concepts. It seems to imply that when Jackson thought up the Mary case, he *had* to have a faint copy of the experience of seeing red. And that seems wrong. But suppose the view is correct. What does that have to do with natural selection?

TOLLENS: Well, suppose that when a person reasons with certain theoretical concepts, his or her thoughts involved phenomenal concepts too. On the "faint copies" view about phenomenal concepts, reasoning with those theoretical concepts would be potentially disastrous. Zoologists might jump out of their chairs every time they think about tiger physiology!

PONENS: And etymologists' skin might crawl when they write articles about cockroaches!

TOLLENS: Right! Being able to reason ourselves into perceptual states would be disadvantageous. So, there are evolutionary reasons to believe that our faculties of reason and perception would develop separately. And there are evolutionary fitness considerations that suggest that these two faculties would have had to develop to be cognitively isolated from each other. Hunter-gatherers who had experiences of tigers whenever they theorized about them wouldn't have lasted long, would they?

PONENS: Maybe not, but your argument has problems. For one thing, you slide rather quickly between perceptual recognitional concepts, which help us avoid predators, and phenomenal concepts, which are all you say

Mary gains. Those two sorts of concepts are, I think, distinct. But I'm willing to put that aside.

TOLLENS: That's generous of you, considering you don't even hint about what the supposed difference is between perceptual and phenomenal concepts.

PONENS: Sarcasm noted. Anyway, suppose you're right and theoretical and phenomenal concepts are cognitively isolated from each other. I don't think that will save your old-fact/new-disguise view anyway.

TOLLENS: I was wondering why you were smiling.

PONENS: I suspect your strategy is a wolf in sheep's clothing.

TOLLENS: I meant it to be a wolf. It's supposed to blow your house down!

PONENS: What I mean is that your strategy won't deliver the goods. What you're saying reminds me of some pretty weak moves Sarah was making last night.

TOLLENS: Such as?

PONENS: Remember when she was arguing against my counterexample to her "Mary gains only abilities" theory? She said some stuff about how my argument ignores how closely imagination and perception are linked in the human brain. And I responded by noting that we can just stipulate that Mary's brain is a bit atypical.

TOLLENS: I was with you on that.

PONENS: Well, the same sort of reply works here. Even if you're right about how our brains evolved, your points don't apply to a Mary who evolved slightly differently.

TOLLENS: Tell me more about this creature.

PONENS: You say that, thanks to natural selection, there's a neural barrier preventing us from reasoning from theoretical concepts to phenomenal concepts. But we could have been wired differently. At least, there could be beings that lack our neural barriers, and for a Mary of that species . . .

TOLLENS: Martian Mary!

PONENS: Sure, Martian Mary. Nothing about the wiring of *her* brain prevents her from reasoning from theoretical to phenomenal concepts.

TOLLENS: Okay. So?

PONENS: So, if the only reason Mary can't deduce the phenomenal truth about seeing red from her prerelease physical knowledge is that her brain's wiring prevents her from doing so, then Martian Mary *can* do that deduction. In that case, she won't have the revelation Mary does when she leaves the black-and-white room. The Martian roses will look just as she expected.

TOLLENS: How is this a problem for my view?

PONENS: Because then the explanatory gap you supposedly accept doesn't exist. On the "neural barriers" view, there's no epistemic gap between the physical and the phenomenal. Or rather, there's no unbridgeable epistemic gap. An ideal reasoner, whose reasoning abilities aren't limited by the contingencies of the human brain, *could* deduce the facts about conscious experience from the physical facts. So, you've slipped from only denying the existence of the metaphysical gap, as you wished to, to denying the existence of the epistemic gap.

TOLLENS: Or, to put it a way that doesn't sound so bad for me, I'm suggesting that the epistemic gap results from a contingent feature of our constitution.

PONENS: Right.

TOLLENS: You act like that's a surprise, but is it really? My basic idea is that there's no gap in reality but only in the way we *know* reality. If you remove all cognitive limitations on knowers, then it's not so surprising if the epistemic gap disappears.

PONENS: But was your intuition about our original Mary case driven by the assumption that she was a normal human being with a set of arcane neural constraints? Did that assumption play a crucial role? I doubt it. Wasn't your intuition instead driven by a more general recognition that it's impossible to learn what it's like to see in color just by reflection on physical information?

TOLLENS: Ponens, I don't know why I have the intuitions I have. But I will say that if you make Mary different enough from people like me, my well of intuitions dries up pretty quickly. I don't know what it's like to be a Martian Mary, and I don't know what to say about her. I'll be satisfied if my theory of phenomenal concepts answers the original argument—the one in which the protagonist is a human being, albeit an exceptionally smart one.

PONENS: To my mind, the argument based on Martian Mary seems no less cogent than the original version. But suit yourself, I guess.

TOLLENS: I will. But let's play your game. Suppose what I said about neural barriers is wrong. Even so, you're making an assumption that I don't have to grant.

PONENS: What's that?

TOLLENS: You're assuming that if the phenomenal truth about color experience can be deduced from the physical truth then Mary can do that deduction.

PONENS: Okay, what's wrong with that?

TOLLENS: I'll get to that. But first let's go back to phenomenal concepts. I think they bear a uniquely close relation to experience. One needn't have any particular type of experience in order to acquire the concept of a table. The same is true of the concept of a salamander and the concept of a number. But one does seem to need to see red in order to have the corresponding phenomenal redness concept—the concept of what it's like to see red. Maybe that's just how phenomenal concepts work.

PONENS: I'm not so sure. What if I've seen dark pink but not red? Can't you sort of darken the color in your mind and thereby figure out what it's like to see red? Wouldn't you then have the phenomenal-redness concept even though you've never seen red?

TOLLENS: Okay, so maybe the experience condition on possessing phenomenal concepts isn't super-strict. One still has to have relevantly *similar* experiences.

PONENS: Even a less strict requirement might not work. Imagine Mary does a science project inside her room. She uses her remarkable physical knowledge to construct a physical duplicate of some woman who has seen red plenty of times. The duplicate would know what it's like to see red, just as I do when I'm not looking at red things or imagining doing so. But unlike me, she wouldn't ever have seen red.

TOLLENS: Okay, look. I'm not sure whether this Frankenmary knows what it's like to see red, though maybe she does. But even *her* phenomenal knowledge has an awful lot to do with having a disposition to enter an experiential state. This business about how *exactly* the experience condition on having phenomenal concepts should be formulated is a nitpicky digression.

PONENS: I like digressions. They're like subplots in movies. Sometimes they're better than the main story line.

TOLLENS: And sometimes they're like commercials.

PONENS: Fair enough.

TOLLENS: Back to my claim, then, which was this: Phenomenal concepts bear a uniquely close relationship to experience and phenomenal properties. Perhaps phenomenal concepts even constitute, or partly constitute, phenomenal properties. But whatever the details, it's hard if not impossible to possess the concept of phenomenal redness without seeing red, weird cases such as Frankenmary notwithstanding.

PONENS: Okay, granted. So what?

TOLLENS: If this is right, then maybe the Mary case isn't a fair test of the epistemic gap. The reason she doesn't know what it's like to see in color before leaving the room isn't that there's an epistemic gap. It's just that she lacks the concepts needed to possess such knowledge.

PONENS: Interesting. So now you're saying that Mary's inability to figure out what it's like to see red before leaving the room has nothing to do with contingent facts about her brain? Martian Mary couldn't do the deduction either?

TOLLENS: Right.

PONENS: Okay, good. I get the point. But I have another worry.

TOLLENS: You don't say!

PONENS: Yes, I think your new view faces a dilemma.

TOLLENS: A dilemma no less! Crikey!

PONENS: Uh-huh. The dilemma concerns what prerelease Mary can figure out, not about color experience, but about phenomenal color *concepts*. Either she can deduce everything about them by theorizing from physical information or she can't.

TOLLENS: True.

PONENS: Well, if she can, she'd make no epistemic progress when she leaves the room.

TOLLENS: Hmmm. So this arm of the dilemma forces me to reject the epistemic gap.

PONENS: Right. Wait! Do dilemmas have arms? I thought they had horns.

TOLLENS: They have both arms and horns. They're like Balrogs.

PONENS: Okay there, Frodo.

TOLLENS: Why can't I dig in my heels and conclude, "So much the worse for the epistemic gap?"

PONENS: You can, but you'll need more ammunition, not just the business about how Mary lacks phenomenal concepts.

TOLLENS: Why?

PONENS: Remember the *Revenge of the Zombies* point? It applies here too.

TOLLENS: Another sequel!

PONENS: Now playing at a theater near you! Phenomenal concepts play the roles formerly played by phenomenal knowledge, but the plot's the same. Even if we give Mary the phenomenal color concepts, she could coherently conceive of a zombie world. And that suggests that, even if she *has* all the relevant concepts, she can't *deduce* the phenomenal truth from the physical truth—despite her limitless logical reasoning ability.

TOLLENS: Damn those zombies.

PONENS: Yep, they're hard to kill. So anyway, that's one arm. On the other arm, suppose Mary can't deduce everything about phenomenal color concepts from the physical information. Now your view allows for Mary's epistemic progress. But it leaves us in essentially the same position we were in before you tried this move about Mary's lacking phenomenal concepts.

TOLLENS: Why is that?

PONENS: Mary knows everything physical and is a flawless reasoner. If there are concepts that are so closely tied to experience that even she can't understand their full nature, then not all features of the mind are objective, as physicalism seems to require. So, the original problem posed by phenomenal properties reemerges at the level of phenomenal concepts.

TOLLENS: Ah, the objectivity bit again.

PONENS: It's back.

TOLLENS: So, a lot depends on two principles. The first is Disguise Depends on Ignorance. The second is the principle that physical truths are objective: In principle, they can be fully understood just through pure reasoning.

PONENS: That's right. Both principles look pretty sturdy to me.

TOLLENS: I have my doubts, especially about the second principle, but I'll let that pass for now.

PONENS: Why? I'm up for it.

TOLLENS: I'm not. My brain is fried. I do want to ask you about one more thing, though. I'm starting to worry that in the past few days we may have been losing the dialectical forest for all the argumentative trees.

PONENS: That's easy to do.

TOLLENS: So we started out with Descartes' argument for dualism.

PONENS: The one Nous liked.

TOLLENS: Right, and then we moved on to the contemporary anti-physicalist arguments. Most of those resemble Descartes' argument pretty closely, no?

PONENS: Yes, though there are important differences. For one thing, Descartes focused on thought more than experience. Also, his argument would establish the existence of a nonphysical soul, whereas the contemporary arguments aim at a weaker conclusion, about physical information or physical properties.

TOLLENS: Okay, but there are also striking similarities. This is clear in the case of the conceivability arguments involving zombies, inverted spectra, and so on. Those arguments and Descartes' all begin with a conceivability claim concerning the mental and the physical. And both then combine that claim with a principle connecting conceivability to metaphysical possibility to draw a conclusion about the nonphysicality of the mental.

PONENS: Yes, that's right. In fact, similar things might be said about the knowledge argument. It too can be seen as relying on a conceivability claim, though more indirectly. This is reasonably clear if we invoke the *Revenge of the Zombies* point. And it's plausible independently. Prerelease, Mary can conceive of what it's like to see red as being this way or that way—her comprehensive physical knowledge doesn't settle the matter. Also, the knowledge argument involves an inference that corresponds, more or less, to the inference from conceivability to possibility that's invoked explicitly by all the conceivability arguments, including Descartes'.

TOLLENS: Okay, good. But I'm surprised you admit that these analogies are legitimate. After all, you agreed that Descartes' argument doesn't work. Didn't Arnauld show that it relies on a mistaken inference?

PONENS: Not exactly. If you'll recall, Arnauld leveled a challenge. He said that conceiving something doesn't indicate its possibility if that conception isn't, in Descartes' phrase, clear and distinct. The challenge was to come up with a single notion of clear-and-distinct conceivability that makes *both* of Descartes' premises plausible: his premise that he can clearly and distinctly conceive of his mind without his body *and* his premise that clear and distinct conceivability entails metaphysical possibility.

TOLLENS: Alright, so it was a challenge, not a refutation. Have we said anything that answers the challenge? I don't think so.

PONENS: We may not have a way to vindicate Descartes' claims, but we do have a way to make something like his "clarity and distinctness" idea a bit more precise. A hypothesis H is clearly and distinctly conceivable if and only if H can't be ruled out by good reasoning—that is, if it's impossible to deduce anything incoherent from H.

TOLLENS: I see. So do you think that would have satisfied Arnauld?

PONENS: Probably not. But he was a twentieth child. Twentieth children are often rather difficult to please, especially after they become philosophers.

TOLLENS: I can imagine. But I'm an only child and I'm not sure I'm convinced, either.

PONENS: Well, only children have issues of their own. Let's sleep on it.

TOLLENS: Yes, let's.

Friday Night

Scene: Ponens and Tollens have their ears up to the air vent located next to the corner where they can be found on any given night.

TOLLENS: Do you hear anything?

PONENS: No, nothing.

TOLLENS: Let me listen. I'm sure I heard a noise coming from that vent.

PONENS: It was probably just the heat kicking in.

TOLLENS: It didn't sound like that. It was a sort of scurrying. I hope it's not rats.

PONENS: Me, too. I don't think I could sleep alongside rats. Present company excluded.

TOLLENS: I don't hear anything now. Maybe I was just hearing things.

PONENS: Good. I think I'm going to go ahead and sleep.

TOLLENS: What? We just got here! Don't you want to talk about consciousness?

PONENS: You aren't sick of that yet?

TOLLENS: No, actually. I'd like to know where you stand, for one thing.

PONENS: I think I've made myself pretty clear. In my view, the anti-physicalist arguments work.

TOLLENS: But those arguments are negative: They conclude that physicalism is false. They don't say what view should replace physicalism. So I'm wondering what your positive position is.

PONENS: Fair enough. I wouldn't want to sell you on a bill of goods that you hadn't inspected thoroughly beforehand.

TOLLENS: I'm not inclined to buy much of what you're selling, but it would help to know exactly what I'm rejecting. My view is that the world is completely physical, but perhaps the alternative isn't as crazy as I think.

PONENS: Maybe not. Often when people hear I reject physicalism, they think I must believe in something supernatural: ghosts that float through the world hurling furniture at unsuspecting landowners . . .

TOLLENS: Or at real estate developers who erect subdivisions over old graveyards.

PONENS: Right. But remember, I don't even believe in souls.

TOLLENS: So, you agree that the mind is the brain?

PONENS: I can probably accept that, as long as you allow that the brain might have nonphysical, phenomenal properties—or nonphysical *qualia,* as they're sometimes called. And I definitely agree with some of your views about explanation. Cognitive states stand a good chance of receiving complete physical explanations, except insofar as those states involve consciousness. In my view, only conscious experience and states involving it resist physical explanation.

TOLLENS: Okay, that's milder than a full-out dualism that embraces souls, but it still sounds strange. I'm picturing a brain dipped in candy-colored sprinkles or something.

PONENS: Mmmm, that's a tasty image. But it's a little off base. Properties aren't like sprinkles. Sprinkles are things, not properties.

TOLLENS: So if that's not the picture, what is?

PONENS: I'm not wedded to any particular metaphysical picture. But an old fashioned example might be useful here. Socrates, apparently, was snub-nosed.

TOLLENS: No kidding. Was that unusual?

PONENS: Apparently you didn't see much of that in ancient Greece. People were always remarking about it. In any case, the snubness was a property of his nose, not a thing sitting on his nose. Some philosophers call properties "modes."

TOLLENS: So why don't you call them modes?

PONENS: Because I don't want to.

TOLLENS: Okay.

PONENS: So the snubness of a nose isn't like sprinkles on ice cream. Suppose you bash Socrates' nose in, as I'm sure some Athenians dreamed of doing. His nose loses its snubness, but it's not as though the snubness falls off into the gutter.

TOLLENS: Alright, I'm with you. No more sprinkles.

PONENS: So properties of consciousness are just that: *properties,* like the snubness of Socrates' nose. But unlike snubness, phenomenal properties, a.k.a. qualia, aren't *physical* properties.

TOLLENS: Why does it mean for a property to be physical?

PONENS: That depends on what "physical" means. For example, suppose "physical" means something fully determined by what physics posits. In that case, snubness would be physical. By contrast, according to nonphysicalists like me, qualia aren't determined by the posits of physics and so aren't physical.

TOLLENS: That does correct the picture I had, but I'm not sure it replaces it with anything. It's not easy for me to see how a physical event such as a brain process could have a nonphysical property.

PONENS: Is it any easier to see how a *non*physical event could have nonphysical qualia? I don't see why it should be.

TOLLENS: You don't? I do. I mean, what if there *were* nonphysical souls? I don't believe in such things. But if they did exist, wouldn't they be precisely the sorts of things that you'd expect to have states with nonphysical qualia?

PONENS: Perhaps, but it's unclear why the *nonphysicality* of souls would help. Saying that souls aren't in space, or that they don't conform to physical laws, doesn't seem relevant. Suppose the science lectures Mary watches on a black-and-white monitor cover not only all physical truths but also everything about the laws governing Cartesian souls. She learns all the physical *and* nonphysical truths that can be learned in that way. Even so, the argument goes through just as in the original version.

TOLLENS: Wait a minute. I thought the knowledge argument was a challenge to *physicalism*. Dualists have to worry about it too?

PONENS: Sort of, depending on the details of their views. Nagel makes the point well in his book, *The View from Nowhere*. Let me go get that.

Ponens searches the shelves for Nagel's book. Meanwhile, Tollens stares at the reflection of his nose in the shiny metal on the side of a carousel. Minutes later, Ponens returns.

TOLLENS: Do you think it's a bit snubby?

PONENS: What?

TOLLENS: My nose. You know, like Socrates'?

PONENS: Oh. No, your nose isn't snubby.

TOLLENS: Not at all?

PONENS: Not at all. Now that we've got that settled, here's the passage I was referring to:

> The main objection to dualism is that it postulates an additional, non-physical substance without explaining how *it* can support subjective mental states whereas the brain can't. Even if we conclude that mental events are not simply physical events, it doesn't follow that we can explain their place in the universe by summoning up a type of substance whose sole function is to provide them with a medium. There are two points here. First, postulating such a substance doesn't explain how it can be the subject of mental states. If there were a thing that lacked mass, energy, and spatial dimensions, would that make it easier to understand how there could be something it was like to *be* that thing? The real difficulty is to make sense of the assignment of essentially subjective states to something which belongs to the objective order. Second, no reason has been given to think that if we could find a place for mental states in the world by attaching them to a non-physical substance, we could not equally well find a place for them in something that also has physical properties.

TOLLENS: Okay, those seem like decent points. Still, someone who buys the anti-physicalist arguments could accept the soul theory.

PONENS: I suppose so, but it certainly isn't mandatory, and it doesn't even seem desirable. I say we have sufficient reason to acknowledge the existence of nonphysical phenomenal properties. But I don't think we should posit other nonphysical phenomena unless further arguments compel us to do so.

TOLLENS: Careful, if you continue thinking along those parsimonious lines, you might end up a physicalist like me!

Ponens: Not likely.

Tollens: I wouldn't be so sure. Your view has some pretty strange consequences.

Ponens: I'm listening.

Tollens: By your own lights, physical phenomena can be explained in entirely physical terms. That's why, on your view, Mary can learn the completed science of color vision without leaving the black-and-white room, right?

Ponens: Yes, that's right.

Tollens: So the nonphysical properties you believe in aren't needed to explain anything physical—including the physical states and physical processes that underlie our cognitive lives?

Ponens: Probably. Otherwise physical science wouldn't even be able to explain everything in its own domain; and that seems unlikely.

Tollens: In that case, what's left for your nonphysical qualia to do? Suppose I burn my hand. I say "Ouch!" and jerk my hand away from the burner. You've admitted that these actions can be fully explained in physical terms. But you also say that the felt quality of my pain is nonphysical. This suggests that the felt quality *doesn't* cause me to say "Ouch!" or move my hand. And that just can't be right. If the phenomenal pain quality isn't the cause of such actions, I begin to doubt that there is such a property. It seems the ultimate unneeded theoretical accessory.

Ponens: Theoretical accessory? You're saying you believe in pain qualia only because of their role in causing your behavior? Have you ever actually been in pain? Forget about whether pain causes behavior. It hurts! Anyway, how do we know that nonphysical qualia don't affect behavior? Maybe physical science doesn't tell the whole story about how physical actions are caused.

Tollens: Hmmm. There are a couple of ways that could work. One is that the physical cause and the phenomenal cause are both needed to bring about physical behavior, as you and I might both be needed to bring a scale to top 400 pounds. In that case, there's joint causation. Physical and phenomenal properties are *both* needed to explain what happens physically. But then physics wouldn't be able to fully explain its own domain. Something nonphysical would be needed. And you don't buy that.

Ponens: Yeah, that's not what I meant to say.

TOLLENS: Well, it sounded a bit like that. Perhaps you mean that some actions have *two* sufficient causes: a phenomenal cause and a physical cause. The felt quality of my pain experience could, on its own, initiate the chain of events leading to my exclaiming "Ouch!" and jerking my hand away from the stove. Also, a physical property of my brain, which co-occurs with the felt quality, could, on its own, initiate the same chain of events. Now that *is* a coincidence!

PONENS: Coincidences aren't impossible.

TOLLENS: No, but it seems doubtful that every time phenomenal properties have physical effects there just happen to be physical properties there producing those same effects. It's like my saying I could lift a thousand pounds all by myself but, coincidentally, every time I "prove" it to you a hulky weightlifter happens to be holding up the same barbell. You'd be rightly skeptical of my boast, wouldn't you?

PONENS: I suppose.

TOLLENS: Well, why shouldn't I be similarly skeptical of your claim about how your beloved nonphysical qualia have physical effects—effects that physical properties would produce anyway?

PONENS: I'm not so sure about your analogy. The Governator and I both lift barbells in the same way. By contrast, maybe phenomenal causation and physical causation work differently. I'm not convinced that the existence of a physical cause excludes the existence of a phenomenal cause, even if the effects are the same. There are tough issues here.

TOLLENS: Why am I not surprised that you'd find even this simple point perplexing? The physical causes of my action are sufficient, all by themselves, to produce that action. There's just no work for nonphysical phenomenal properties to do.

PONENS: That seems suspicious. You seem to be assuming a specific model of causation, on which only so much energy is needed to get the job done: Because the physical cause expends sufficient energy to cause my action, the phenomenal cause is left without any need to expend any energy it might have. That, anyway, is what the work metaphor suggests to me. But that model may not be appropriate to the case at hand.

TOLLENS: I'm not sure my conclusion depends on any particular model here. I can make my point logically, without reference to models. If one thing is sufficient for another, then nothing else is needed. And if the phenomenal isn't metaphysically necessary for the existence of the physical, as your zombie argument has it, and there's a sufficient physical cause for every physical event, then nothing phenomenal is causally necessary for any physical event.

PONENS: Maybe so, but it doesn't follow that there's no sense in which the phenomenal is causally *relevant* to the physical. Perhaps it is, on some models of causation.

TOLLENS: Do you have such a model in mind?

PONENS: Admittedly no, not at this point.

TOLLENS: Then you'll forgive me if I don't hold my breath?

PONENS: Fair enough. I guess I need to think more about this. Anyway, suppose you're right: Nonphysical phenomenal properties would have no physical effects. What would be so bad about that? Maybe such properties are epiphenomenal: They have physical causes but no physical effects. Jackson defended that view in the article in which he introduced the Mary case. He even called his article "Epiphenomenal Qualia."

TOLLENS: Wait, let me get this straight. You're taking seriously the idea that phenomenal properties don't affect the physical world at all?

PONENS: I suppose.

TOLLENS: That's nuts. And doesn't your own argument assume that phenomenal properties have physical effects? On your view, don't phenomenal properties cause Mary's "Aha!" reaction when she finally sees red and learns what it's like to have such an experience?

PONENS: Actually, I left that issue open. Phenomenal properties—color qualia—figure crucially in Mary's increase in knowledge. That much is true. But do they *cause* her to perform a physical action—to say "Aha," assuming she does so? Maybe, but I want to remain noncommittal here.

TOLLENS: But your whole argument is based on an intuition about the Mary case. And isn't the idea that color qualia fail to cause her "Aha!" reaction flatly counterintuitive?

PONENS: Maybe, but I never said common sense gets everything right.

TOLLENS: Well, I certainly agree with that last point. Still, if a theory posits a property that literally does nothing, something must be wrong with that theory.

PONENS: What do you mean by saying a property *does nothing*? Do you mean it has no *physical* effects?

TOLLENS: I guess.

PONENS: In that case, I'm not so sure about your principle. Even if phenomenal properties don't have physical effects, they do other explanatory work. They explain the way certain states feel. They explain the "what it's like."

TOLLENS: But doesn't this causal conundrum suggest to you that you've gone astray? If phenomenal properties wind up doing nothing except for sitting around as feelings they're, to say the least, poorly integrated into the rest of nature. That makes for an inelegant picture—not much better than the one painted by crusty old Descartes.

PONENS: Yeah, I see that. But epiphenomenalists might take issue with you here. They'd ask: Why should we expect phenomenal properties to be seamlessly integrated into the causal fabric of the world?

TOLLENS: Good question. I guess the point concerns simplicity and elegance. Complexity and inelegance lowers the likelihood that a theory is true. And epiphenomenalism has those deficiencies. It paints an overly fragmented picture of the world. If we had compelling evidence or arguments for that picture, then we might have to accept it. But we lack both.

PONENS: I think you're being too dismissive here. There are considerations that support the epiphenomenalist's skepticism about the physical effects of qualia.

TOLLENS: Such as?

PONENS: For one thing, there's an evolutionary consideration, similar to one you mentioned last night. If you think about it, the survival benefits of perception and sensation don't stem from what it's like to perceive and sense. What matters for survival are the associated functions—avoidance behavior, etc. As long as burning your hand causes you to enter a state that leads you to avoid doing that again, it doesn't matter exactly how the state feels phenomenally, or even whether the state has a phenomenal feel at all. Evolution would favor the state that produces the behavior, regardless of any associated qualia.

TOLLENS: So you're saying that we shouldn't expect phenomenal properties to cause behavior that evolved through natural selection—behavior such as avoiding contact with extremely hot surfaces?

PONENS: Well, the point is that the phenomenal qualities associated with evolved behavioral traits aren't essential to those traits; the traits might have evolved in the same way even if no phenomenal qualities were associated with them.

TOLLENS: I think that gets it backwards. Instead we should say that, given the way natural selection works, we shouldn't expect our mental states to have any properties that lack physical effects.

PONENS: I don't know about that. Not all physical traits exist because they confer survival advantages. Some are by-products of adaptations, not adaptations themselves. So, why think phenomenal properties can't be by-products? Also, there's evidence that qualia don't play the causal roles commonly ascribed to them.

TOLLENS: Such as?

PONENS: One relevant experiment is described in a book that Sarah left behind. Here's the description:

> Each subject was asked to reach suddenly for a given target image or object. After the reaching movement began but before the target was touched, the location of the target was shifted. The subjects altered the direction of their reaching movements in "mid-stream" to touch the target at its new location. The interesting point here is that the subjects were not aware of making the midstream change in direction; the alteration was done unconsciously.

TOLLENS: Interesting. But what does that prove?

PONENS: It suggests that there might be something wrong with the idea that the visual qualia associated with seeing the target caused the subjects to point as they did.

TOLLENS: Huh.

PONENS: That experiment and others suggest that, even when there's conscious awareness of a change in the environment, this awareness occurs only *after* the body has begun the process of moving and adapting itself. Apparently it takes more time for stimuli to register in consciousness than to trigger the bodily response. Or at least, that happens sometimes. In such cases, the phenomenal properties associated with the stimulus don't seem to cause our behavioral response, at least not in the way we tend to assume.

TOLLENS: That's interesting, but I'm not terribly surprised. If you've ever played a quick sport such as squash or racquetball . . .

PONENS: Or table tennis, the world's quickest and greatest sport.

TOLLENS: You really need to get out more, Ponens.

PONENS: I would, but the wind outside messes up the game.

TOLLENS: Um, right. Well, as I was saying, if you become good at those sports, you end up reacting with precision and skill before you have time to consciously register what you're doing.

PONENS: That's true.

TOLLENS: Still, none of this proves that qualia lack physical effects completely. The experiments actually seem to presuppose that qualia have *some* physical effects.

PONENS: Why?

TOLLENS: Presumably the scientists need evidence of the moment when an experience begins, in order to establish that it lags behind the bodily reaction.

PONENS: True. Usually the subjects are asked to vocalize or press a button the moment they become aware of an environmental change.

TOLLENS: Well, there you go. That presupposes some causal link between conscious awareness and vocalization of that awareness. To get the result you want, I think you'd need an experiment that establishes the onset of the relevant experiences more directly—without the intermediary of vocalizations and such. And how are you going to pull that one off?

PONENS: Maybe scientists could determine that by looking for neural correlates of the experiences. Correlation isn't causation.

TOLLENS: But won't finding such neural correlates raise similar issues?

PONENS: Maybe. Anyway, I don't claim these or any other experiments establish epiphenomenalism. But I do claim they should make us question our ordinary assumptions about how phenomenal properties affect the physical world. And if we give up those assumptions, epiphenomenalism may not seem so implausible.

TOLLENS: Okay, but admit it, the ideas you're advancing are strange.

PONENS: Granted. But think about how strange the world is from the perspective of basic physics—how different the explanations physics provides are from the way we think about cause and effect in everyday life. Given that strangeness, can we really trust what common sense has to say about the causal features of consciousness?

TOLLENS: Hold on, now. I think science is definitely on my side on this matter.

PONENS: Really, this isn't so clear. . . .

TOLLENS: Wait!

PONENS: What?! Don't startle me. What is it?

TOLLENS: I heard something in the vent again.

PONENS: Oh, ignore it. Do you agree with what I've been saying, or what?

TOLLENS: No, I don't. I think you underestimate the difficulties involved in causally isolating phenomenal properties from physical actions.

PONENS: How so?

TOLLENS: Think about it. If beliefs, judgments, and their vocalizations all have complete physical explanations, and qualia are nonphysical, then even our judgments about conscious experiences aren't caused by qualia! Even your zeal in believing in nonphysical properties has a complete physical explanation—an explanation in which, given your view, consciousness itself plays no role whatsoever! That seems utterly intolerable. The reason we're having this debate is that we're supposed to *know* about these phenomenal properties, right? But how can we know about them if they can't even affect our *beliefs* about them?

PONENS: I admit that doesn't look good. My view seems to imply that there could be a zombie version of myself saying the same things I'm saying, or at least making the same noises and such. Chalmers points this out in his book *The Conscious Mind.* I was reading it the other night, and it's still here in my pillow pile. Here's the passage:

> To see the problem in a particularly vivid way, think of my zombie twin in the universe next door. He talks about conscious experience all the time—in fact, he seems obsessed by it. He spends ridiculous amounts of time hunched over a computer, writing chapter after chapter on the mysteries of consciousness. He often comments on the pleasure he gets from certain sensory qualia, professing a particular love for deep greens and purples. He frequently gets into arguments with zombie materialists, arguing that their position cannot do justice to the realities of conscious experience.
>
> And yet he has no conscious experience at all! In his universe the materialists are right and he is wrong. Most of his claims about conscious experience are utterly false. But there is certainly a physical or functional explanation of why he makes

the claims he makes. After all, his universe is fully law-governed, and no events therein are miraculous, so there must be *some* explanation of his claims. But such an explanation must ultimately be in terms of physical processes and laws, for these are the *only* processes and laws in his universe.

TOLLENS: That seems a particularly bad consequence of your view.

PONENS: It's bad, but I don't think it's fatal. If you think it's fatal, then you're making additional assumptions. I suspect you're assuming that to think or know about some property, you must be in causal contact with that property.

TOLLENS: How else could you think or know about something?

PONENS: I'm not sure, but consider mathematical knowledge or knowledge of logic. I know that 7 + 5 = 12, but am I in causal contact with numbers? I doubt it. I know that *q* follows deductively from the conjunction of *p* and *if p then q*. But am I in causal contact with the laws of deductive logic? That seems unlikely. Causal theories don't seem to apply to these judgments. Maybe they don't apply to judgments about one's own conscious experience either.

TOLLENS: That analogy is questionable. Math and logic are abstract in a way that consciousness isn't. Anyway, even if the analogy works, I don't think it provides much comfort.

PONENS: Why not?

TOLLENS: Your view about the nature of consciousness forces you to take an odd position on knowledge of and reference to consciousness. In my book, that counts against your view.

PONENS: Fair enough. I admit that you've introduced a bullet that I'll have to bite. But I'm not sure it's unbiteable.

TOLLENS: Better be careful. Biting bullets can blow your head off.

PONENS: True. But we still have the anti-physicalist arguments on our hands. You can't dismiss an argument just because its conclusion has undesirable consequences. You still have to show what's wrong with the argument.

TOLLENS: Granted.

PONENS: Even so, I do see that physicalism has various advantages, and I'd like my view to preserve as many of those as possible. In particular, I'd prefer it if I could accept some nonphysicalist version of monism.

TOLLENS: As opposed to dualism?

PONENS: Yes. Dualists have to worry about integrating two fundamentally distinct sorts of phenomena into a coherent picture. Monists, including physicalists, don't have that problem. Monism can be rather elegant. And elegance is important.

TOLLENS: I'd find that point more persuasive it if came from someone whose t-shirt wasn't on backwards.

PONENS: It is?

TOLLENS: I'm afraid so. Anyway, I couldn't agree more with what you say about monism; that's the sort of consideration I've been pushing all week. Do I hear somebody coming around to my view?

PONENS: I'm afraid not. First of all, there are other forms of monism besides physicalism. Idealism, for example, as promoted by good old Bishop Berkeley, held that the world was entirely mental.

TOLLENS: Anyone who believes that theory has certainly gone mental.

PONENS: Don't be so dismissive. Berkeley had arguments for his view.

TOLLENS: I'll bet they were interesting. Insanity often is.

PONENS: Now you're just baiting me. Anyway, I'm not saying idealism is true. I don't think it is. My point is only that idealism is a form of monism that's distinct from physicalism.

TOLLENS: Fine, but if you reject idealism and physicalism, then how can you be a monist?

PONENS: Well, there's also the view that the physical and the phenomenal are both manifestations of a single, more basic sort of property. That view is called "neutral monism."

TOLLENS: Interesting. But is neutral monism any better than dualism? Don't similar problems arise, about how the two distinct manifestations are connected?

PONENS: Yeah, that's a problem. But there's a related view that's consistent with the anti-physicalist arguments and has some of the main advantages of monism. Actually, there are a couple of views that fit that description. One is sometimes called "panpsychism" because it implies that phenomenal properties are ubiquitous: They serve as the categorical basis of physical dispositions.

TOLLENS: What on Earth does that mean? What's a categorical . . . hey!

PONENS: Huh?

TOLLENS: Didn't you hear that?

PONENS: Are you still listening to that stupid air vent?

TOLLENS: Alright, forget it. I must be getting overtired or something. I'm going to sleep.

PONENS: But I haven't told you how I can have my cake and eat it too.

TOLLENS: You can be a glutton tomorrow. Right now I'm going to dreamland before I start not only hearing things but seeing them too.

PONENS: 'Night, then.

TOLLENS: Yeah, 'night.

Saturday

Scene: Early Saturday morning. Ponens and Tollens are sleeping near their usual corner when banging and sliding noises in the air vent wake them up.

TOLLENS: What the . . . ?

PONENS: What!? Mother? Daddy? Uncle Gus?

TOLLENS: It's me, Ponens! Don't tell me you didn't hear *that*!

PONENS: No, no, I heard it. What did I hear?

There is an insistent banging on the vent cover.

PONENS: Maybe we should get away from that thing.

The banging and scampering continue until the vent cover pops out, followed by a head almost completely covered in dark grizzled hair.

TOLLENS & PONENS: Aaaargh!

ANIMUS: Don't scream, don't be scared! I'm not here to hurt you.

TOLLENS: What in the . . . ? Who are you? What are you doing in the vent?

ANIMUS: They call me Animus. I'm a ventilator troll.

PONENS: You're a troll?

ANIMUS: No, not really. But I live in here.

PONENS: You live in the vent?

ANIMUS: Not just in the vents, but in the ductwork and crawlspaces of the library. So I've been thinking about the argument you were having earlier, and I have to say . . .

PONENS: You've been listening to us?

ANIMUS: Well, I'm as curious as the next guy.

TOLLENS: Wait. First things first. How do you eat? How do you, um, take care of yourself?

ANIMUS: I have a system. I'd rather not discuss it.

PONENS: Let's not make him mad.

ANIMUS: So I've been listening, and I agree with whoever said that everything is alive.

TOLLENS: I don't think anyone said that.

PONENS: Well, I did mention panpsychism.

ANIMUS: Right! I'm a panpsychist.

PONENS: That's the view that mentality pervades everything, down to the basic level of reality.

ANIMUS: You bet!

TOLLENS: Are you talking about the view that everything is made of ideas, for which that Bishop guy supposedly gave such "interesting" arguments?

PONENS: Berkeley. And shut up about his arguments; you haven't even heard them. Anyway, the panpsychist view I have in mind isn't a version of idealism. On this view, phenomenal properties aren't physical properties, and physical properties aren't phenomenal properties. Also, everything has properties of both kinds.

TOLLENS: There are physical and phenomenal properties, and neither type of property reduces to the other?

PONENS: Right.

TOLLENS: Then it's dualism, not monism.

PONENS: Well, it could be a version of neutral monism. It would be, if the physical and phenomenal are construed as manifestations of a single, more basic property. You can call panpsychism dualism if you like, but it still has one of the principal advantages of monism. On monistic theories such as physicalism and idealism, everything is composed of the same sorts of basic components. And that's elegant. Panpsychism is elegant in the same way—whether or not it's construed as a form of monism.

TOLLENS: Wait a minute. I've read that some physicists think much of the universe consists of "dark matter," stuff that's composed of hypothetical new particles called "axions"—"new" in the sense of being unfamiliar: They don't compose things with which we're acquainted. So any view that says everything is composed of the same stuff may be false for straightforward empirical reasons.

PONENS: Yeah, I've read about dark matter too. But I take it that, despite their novelty, axions fall into the same general category as other, more familiar particles physics postulates. What I said is unaffected by the dark matter hypothesis. I said that monism is elegant because it implies that everything is composed of the same *sorts* of basic components. And panpsychism has that implication, too. On panpsychism, I, Fifi, and that bookshelf are all made of the same sorts of basic components.

ANIMUS: That's right! It's all alive, man! You, Fifi, the books, everything! Take these air ducts, for example. Can't you hear them breathing? Sometimes I think the furnace is my only friend.

TOLLENS: I see. Warm-hearted, I take it.

ANIMUS: Exactly! So warm!

TOLLENS: This reminds me of something I read for an ancient history class. Lucretius, one of the founders of what's called "atomism," ridiculed the sort of view you two are talking about. I'll go see if I can find the book we used.

While Tollens searches for the book, Animus stares at the wall. Ponens notices Animus' concerned look but decides to remain silent. Tollens returns three minutes later.

TOLLENS: Okay, I found it. Here's the fragment I mentioned:

> Again, if we are to account for the power of sensation possessed by animate creatures in general by attributing sentience to their atoms, what of those atoms that specifically compose the human race? Presumably they are not merely sentient, but also shake their sides with uproarious guffaws and besprinkle their cheeks with dewy teardrops and even discourse profoundly and at length about the composition of the universe and proceed to ask of what elements they are themselves composed.

PONENS: Actually, panpsychism need not imply any of that. Nor need it imply that the air ducts breathe or that the furnace is warm-hearted.

TOLLENS: Why not?

PONENS: Panpsychism implies that the furnace has phenomenal states but not necessarily states familiar to us.

TOLLENS: What sort of phenomenal states do they have?

PONENS: Panpsychists might argue that the simpler the system, the simpler its phenomenal states. But that's guesswork. Anyway, there's a related view that doesn't lend itself to ridicule in quite the same way.

TOLLENS: Do tell.

PONENS: The view I have in mind takes its cue from a connection between two problems. One, which we've been discussing, is how to integrate nonphysical qualia into nature. The other is a problem in an area that may seem far afield: the philosophy of physics.

TOLLENS: Interesting. Go on.

PONENS: Physics characterizes its basic properties in dispositional terms.

TOLLENS: English, please.

PONENS: Think about mass, charge, and so on. Such properties are ultimately characterized in terms of dispositions to attract particles, to repel particles, and so on.

TOLLENS: Okay.

PONENS: Well, a question arises about what *grounds* such dispositions. To serve that purpose, we need *non*dispositional or *categorical* properties.

TOLLENS: You're losing me.

PONENS: Okay, take the windows in the library. They're fragile, right?

ANIMUS: Actually, they stand up to quite a bit.

PONENS: Still, they're somewhat fragile. This means roughly that they're disposed to break when hit with enough force, in normal conditions.

TOLLENS: Fair enough.

PONENS: Well, there must be something about the glass that accounts for the windows' fragility.

TOLLENS: Sure. Something about its physical composition. Its atomic structure, for example.

PONENS: Right. But the funny thing is that physics describes the features that make glass brittle in terms of dispositions as well. Ultimately, atomic structure is also explained in terms of more basic dispositions. And the same holds for the features that ground those more basic dispositions.

When it comes to the categorical properties that *ultimately* underlie physical dispositions, physics is silent.

TOLLENS: Huh.

PONENS: There's a nice passage on this by the philosopher Simon Blackburn. I think I have the article in my bag . . .

TOLLENS: Excuse me, Animus, but I think you're drooling.

ANIMUS: Ah, sorry. But hands are in the vent, head's out. What am I supposed to do?

TOLLENS: Good point.

PONENS: Here's the quotation:

> When we think of categorical grounds, we are apt to think of a spatial configuration of things—hard, massy, shaped things resisting penetration and displacement by others of their kind. But the categorical credentials of any item on this list are poor. Resistance is *par excellence* dispositional; extension is only of use, as Leibniz insisted, if there is some other property whose instancing defines the boundaries; hardness goes with resistance, and mass is knowable only by its dynamical effects. Turn up the magnitude and we find things like electrical charge at a point, or rather varying over a region, but the magnitude of a field at a region is known only through its effect on other things in spatial relations to that region. A region with charge is very different from a region without: perhaps different enough to explain all we could ever know about nature. It differs in precisely its dispositions or powers. But science finds only dispositional properties all the way down.

PONENS: So, physical science characterizes its basic properties in purely dispositional terms.

TOLLENS: I can see that. But what's the problem, exactly?

PONENS: The problem is that the picture that results is bizarrely empty. If physics describes everything completely, then we get a world of pure dispositions, with no underlying categorical properties to ground them. The world consists of structure, dynamics, and nothing else.

TOLLENS: Structure and dynamics? You've got to cool it with the jargon.

PONENS: Sorry, but these concepts are useful. Think of it this way. To fully describe something's causal role, you need only to describe how that thing fits into a system. Fitting into a system has two aspects: structure and dynamics. Structure is, roughly, how the thing relates to the other components of the system. And how those relations change over time—those are its dynamics.

TOLLENS: That's pretty abstract.

PONENS: Okay, take mass. Physics describes mass as the quantity of matter as determined from its weight. But that comes down to a disposition: the propensity to be accelerated in certain ways by certain forces and under certain conditions, in the system we call the physical universe. That's what mass *is,* as far as physics is concerned.

TOLLENS: Okay, that helps.

PONENS: Good. The point appears to generalize. Physics seems to describe *all* of its basic properties in terms of structure and dynamics.

TOLLENS: Okay. So?

PONENS: So, if the complete physical description of the world leaves nothing out, then the world is nothing but structure. Or nothing but structure and changes in that structure.

TOLLENS: Okay but, again, what's the problem?

PONENS: The problem is that, intuitively, it seems that there should be more than structure: there should be something that *has* structure! On this picture, a basic property in physics consists in structural relations to other properties, and those other properties in turn consist in structural relations to other properties, and so on and so forth—forever! The same goes for chemistry and neuroscience. As Blackburn puts it, science finds only dispositions all the way down. All we get are pure relations, pure dispositions. But what stands in all those relations? What has the structure? What grounds the dispositions? There should be categorical, nonstructural features—features that fill in the structure with content.

TOLLENS: Yeah, I guess that sounds intuitive. But maybe intuition is wrong. What does any of this have to do with consciousness anyway?

PONENS: It seems one thing to grant that *physical* properties are ultimately dispositional, along the lines Blackburn describes. But extending this idea to *phenomenal* properties seems unacceptable. Phenomenal properties aren't merely dispositional; they're not just aspects of structure or dynamics. The property of feeling a certain way doesn't boil down to how one thing relates to something else, or how one state causes another. There's something it's like to be in that state.

TOLLENS: Okay, let's say I grant that. This leads to panpsychism . . . how, exactly?

PONENS: As I said earlier, we have two problems. In the philosophy of physics, there's *the problem of emptiness*. We need categorical properties to underlie basic physical dispositions—properties to be the *relata,* the things that stand in basic physical relations. And in the philosophy of consciousness, there's *the problem of integration*. Where do phenomenal properties fit within the natural order? How can they be integrated into a world that's otherwise completely describable in terms of physical, dispositional properties? See where I'm heading?

TOLLENS: I do, actually. So you have physical properties, which physics describes in dispositional terms, and you have phenomenal properties, which present themselves as categorical properties—as they are in themselves.

PONENS: And dispositions need categorical bases, so . . .

TOLLENS: So physics got its chocolate in consciousness' peanut butter!

PONENS: Right! Phenomenal properties are the categorical bases of physical dispositions. This solves both problems in one go. Physical properties get the categorical grounding that they need, and phenomenal properties are fully integrated into nature. Pretty neat, eh?

TOLLENS: Pretty *wacko,* I'd say. How could a phenomenal property ground the fragility of the window? Also, on this view consciousness would be everywhere, even in vast regions of seemingly lifeless space.

ANIMUS: That's it! That's it exactly! See! I told you everything was alive!

TOLLENS: You're drooling again.

ANIMUS: Sorry. I just get excited sometimes.

TOLLENS: Don't you think the furnace might be getting lonely? Maybe you'd better check on it.

ANIMUS: Ooh, right you are. I'd better go.

PONENS: That might be best.

ANIMUS: Yes. And if Joe comes, don't tell him you saw me.

Animus ducks back into the ventilator shaft. After some banging and shuffling, he is gone.

PONENS: Who's this Joe?

TOLLENS: I wouldn't worry about it. It's probably the sliding stool. That Animus guy is nuts. So do you believe that line about phenomenal properties grounding physical properties?

PONENS: No.

TOLLENS: I'm glad to hear it. One ventilator troll is enough.

PONENS: It seems unlikely that rocks, chairs, and atoms are conscious.

TOLLENS: Or broccoli. This could send vegetarians into a tailspin.

PONENS: And make broccoli more appealing to sadistic nonvegetarians.

TOLLENS: Are you really taking that grizzly ventilator troll's views seriously? Everything is alive?

PONENS: Life is another matter. Having phenomenal states doesn't imply being alive. I'd say being alive is roughly a matter of being able to perform certain functions, such as reproduction and growth through metabolism. I see no reason to suspect that rocks have baby rocks.

TOLLENS: Smashy smashy!

PONENS: I doubt even *Animus* would say that rocks copulate with sledgehammers.

TOLLENS: Okay, but isn't it equally crazy to suppose that rocks have conscious states?

PONENS: Actually, no! I don't see how we can definitively rule out the possibility that every physical system has some phenomenal features, even if those features are rudimentary in many cases.

TOLLENS: Watch out, you're going to start drooling soon.

PONENS: Look, all I'm saying is that we can't definitively rule out panpsychism.

TOLLENS: Okay, fair enough, but we were discussing which view you believe, not views you consider remote possibilities.

PONENS: Actually, we were sleeping. It's 4:00 A.M.

TOLLENS: I meant last night. Anyway, are you ever going to put your cards on the table?

PONENS: I guess I'm sympathetic to a view that's similar to panpsychism, though I admit the view is underdeveloped.

TOLLENS: If it's at all plausible, it can't be too similar to panpsychism.

PONENS: The panpsychist view is implausible because it implies that rocks, atoms, and quarks all have experiences, right?

TOLLENS: That's one major problem, yes.

PONENS: But it could be that there are nonphenomenal properties that do the work the panpsychist assigns to phenomenal properties. These would be *proto*phenomenal properties: nonphenomenal properties that combine in certain ways to constitute phenomenal properties. Protophenomenal properties are like phenomenal properties in that they're not, or not wholly, structural or dynamic. Protophenomenal properties might both ground physical, dispositional properties and be components of consciousness as we know it. It's not panpsychism: It's pan*proto*psychism.

TOLLENS: I'm not sure panprotopsychism sounds much better than Sir Drool-a-Lot's view.

PONENS: Why not? Talk about elegance! This view solves the problem of emptiness and the problem of integration in one go. Plus, it has the advantage associated with monism that we mentioned last night: It uses a single set of tools to explain everything. And it doesn't go off the deep end into full-fledged panpsychism. Physical dispositions are grounded, consciousness is part of nature, and rocks aren't conscious. That's a lot of explanatory power!

TOLLENS: Sure. Plenty of explanatory power as long as you don't mind having as your basis of explanation something we don't know, and perhaps can't know, anything about. And how on Earth is this supposed to work? How do these so-called protophenomenal properties ground physical dispositional properties, such as mass? And how do protophenomenal properties combine to yield any phenomenal properties, let alone familiar ones?

PONENS: I don't know. Those are serious problems. But maybe they can be solved. We've just gotten to the point where we're considering accepting the existence of protophenomenal properties. Maybe we'll learn more about them as the panprotopsychist theory develops. They presumably figure into laws concerning the relationship between the physical and the phenomenal. If we figure out those laws, we'd learn quite a lot about the protophenomenal.

TOLLENS: That seems *ridiculously* speculative.

PONENS: Perhaps, but the arguments that led us here indicate that we know little about how consciousness relates to physical phenomena, at the most basic level. At this point, we shouldn't be dismissive of speculative theories, even if they sound crazy—as long as they show some promise.

TOLLENS: I guess that's right. But to take theories as wild as panprotopsychism seriously, I'd need to know more. What does this theory entail about the anti-physicalist arguments? Which step does it deny?

PONENS: If the arguments are properly formulated, panprotopsychists need not reject them at all.

TOLLENS: But didn't you say that panprotopsychism isn't necessarily a form of dualism? And weren't the arguments we've been debating arguments for dualism?

PONENS: They're often used that way, but they're better understood as arguments against *physicalism as traditionally conceived*. Panprotopsychism questions traditional physicalism no less than dualism does. Granted, we might regard protophenomenal properties as physical properties because of their close relationship to the sorts of properties physics characterizes. If we do, then the panprotopsychist should say that Mary doesn't know everything physical before she leaves the room. The science lectures she sees on black-and-white television inform her about only some of the physical properties: the dispositional ones, not the categorical ones. She learns everything about structure and dynamics, but this doesn't include everything physical in a broader sense of the term "physical."

TOLLENS: Right.

PONENS: But that's only if we decide to call protophenomenal properties physical. We might instead decide to restrict the physical to the structural and dynamical. In that case, Mary's black-and-white science lessons would teach her all physical truths, without exception. And if the physical is understood in this more narrow way, then the panprotopsychist will likely accept the knowledge argument, since on panprotopsychism the phenomenal truths aren't entailed by the structural and dynamic truths alone.

TOLLENS: I see. So, a panprotopsychist might say either that prerelease Mary doesn't know all the physical truths or that she does. If the physical truths include truths involving protophenomenal properties, then she doesn't know those physical truths until she leaves the room. If instead the physical truths include only the structural and dynamic truths, then she knows all physical truths while still in the room. Either way, she learns further truths when she leaves. In short, on this view there's more to the world than physical truths conceived in the traditional way. Is that right?

PONENS: Exactly.

TOLLENS: So what about your friends the zombies? Are they still metaphysically possible?

PONENS: As with the knowledge argument, what the panprotopsychist says here will depend on whether protophenomenal properties are considered physical. If the physical includes only the structural and dynamic, then protophenomenal properties aren't physical. And in that case, the panprotopsychist would presumably hold that zombies are metaphysically possible.

TOLLENS: And if the physical includes the protophenomenal?

PONENS: Then zombies aren't metaphysically possible: Any world that duplicates *all* the physical properties, including the protophenomenal ones, is automatically a world with consciousness. The zombie world seems possible only because we ignore certain physical properties, namely, the categorical, protophenomenal ones.

TOLLENS: So, is panprotopsychism a form of physicalism or what?

PONENS: Or what. It's like physicalism in some ways, but not in others. Even on this version, a consciousness-free world that's *structurally* identical to ours would be metaphysically possible. And that result is incompatible with traditional forms of physicalism.

TOLLENS: Wait—are your precious categorical properties physical or not? By what you just said, that seems to be the crucial question for you.

PONENS: I think calling protophenomenal properties "physical" can mislead. That aside, I don't think much of substance turns on whether the categorical properties are considered physical. The issue is largely terminological.

TOLLENS: But doesn't that so-called terminological issue determine whether physicalism is true or false?

PONENS: Whether physicalism is true or false depends partly on what we choose to mean by "physical." Whatever choice we make, the knowledge argument and the conceivability argument go through. They show that consciousness is something over and above structure and dynamics. That's the crucial result, and it holds whatever we choose to mean by "physical."

TOLLENS: Okay, but let's go back to one of the problems for panprotopsychism I mentioned earlier: How do panprotopsychists squeeze consciousness out of protoconsciousness? You said that's an unsolved problem for the view, right?

PONENS: Yes. It's sometimes called "the combination problem." Solving it will require a lot more theorizing.

TOLLENS: Scientific theories can be tested. How could you test a theory designed to solve the combination problem?

PONENS: Maybe we'll know when a reasonable hypothesis is proposed.

TOLLENS: No, look, you're missing something obvious. You portray the so-called combination problem as merely a challenge—as a reason to further develop the panprotopsychist theory. But really, the problem indicates a basic flaw in the theory: The theory just replaces one mystery with another.

PONENS: Why do you say that?

TOLLENS: Look at it this way. A large part of why we have a difficult time seeing how prerelease Mary could figure out what it's like to see red is that we can't see how to deduce phenomenal information from nonphenomenal information. But this intuition is just as strong when we apply it to so-called protophenomenal information. The intuition is that Mary can't deduce what it's like to see red from nonphenomenal information. It's neither here nor there whether the nonphenomenal information is the sort typically described by physics or the sort described by your I-know-not-what-ology.

PONENS: I think you may be assuming that protophenomenal information is just more structural information. That's a natural assumption, since protophenomenal properties are just theoretical posits, and usually theoretical posits are described in structural terms. Nevertheless, these properties aren't structural, at least not wholly. I do see your point, though. Without solving the combination problem, panprotopsychism looks more than a bit mysterious. But again, I don't see why the problem can't eventually be solved.

TOLLENS: Yeah, that's what you said about the problems associated with causation. Speaking of which, how does this view fare on that score? I don't understand how phenomenal properties could have physical effects, on the panprotopsychist view. But it's a little confusing because they're not simply left out either.

PONENS: That's right. On this view, the *components* of phenomenal properties play a role in grounding physical, dispositional properties. That role is important. But it's played by protophenomenal properties, not full-blown qualia. And it must be admitted, on this view neither phenomenal nor protophenomenal properties play the roles in mental-physical causation that common sense assigns to consciousness.

TOLLENS: Actually, on this view, it seems that the dispositional physical properties do all the work. The fact that they harbor some phenomenal or protophenomenal seed seems irrelevant to the way that our brains and bodies work.

Suddenly, a man wearing a brown jumpsuit and waving a mop jumps from between the stacks.

EPISTEIN: Gotcha!

TOLLENS & PONENS: Aaaargh!

TOLLENS: Watch that mop, man! Who the hell are you?

EPISTEIN: Joe Epistein. I work here.

PONENS: Ah, that figures.

EPISTEIN: You're not who I thought I'd find here. Who are you?

PONENS: We're students.

TOLLENS: Grad students.

PONENS: We got locked in.

EPISTEIN: Yeah, I'll bet. Looks like you guys have set up shop. You've got a makeshift pillow made from books and—is that a toothbrush?

TOLLENS: I carry mine everywhere. You never know. Besides, we're not bothering anyone.

PONENS: We're actually being quite studious. We're discussing some deep philosophical problems.

EPISTEIN: Philosophy, huh? Is that like psychology?

PONENS: Not really, though as it happens we were talking about the mind—the nature of consciousness.

TOLLENS: Yeah, we were debating whether consciousness is physical.

EPISTEIN: You think you're figuring that out here in the corner of the library?

PONENS: I don't know if we're figuring it out.

EPISTEIN: I'll bet you're not. Some things we just can't wrap our minds around, no matter how smart we are. I think you're wasting your time. What happened to that vent cover?

TOLLENS: Nothing. It was like that when we got here.

EPISTEIN: You haven't heard anything from up there, have you? Smelled anything?

PONENS: Well, there was a smell downstairs.

TOLLENS: Nope, nothing.

A metallic creaking is heard in the distance.

EPISTEIN: That's him! You two sit tight. I'll be back in a second.

Joe Epistein runs off, swinging his mop.

PONENS: I think we should leave.

TOLLENS: Nah, he said to sit tight.

PONENS: I guess he'll throw us out either way.

TOLLENS: Yeah. You know, after all of our hemming and hawing, old Joe might have stated the safest view I've heard so far.

PONENS: Joe had a view?

TOLLENS: Sure! He didn't spell it out, but the idea that we can't understand the relationship between consciousness and the physical isn't all that crazy. Maybe we're just not in a position to understand this, at least not yet.

PONENS: Speak for yourself.

TOLLENS: Oh, c'mon. Actually, I can see two different views Joe might have had in mind. One is that in thinking about this problem we're like monkeys contemplating calculus. Our brains just aren't up to the task.

PONENS: What's the other view?

TOLLENS: It's similar but less pessimistic. Maybe we're more like scientists in the nineteenth century contemplating the relationship between chemistry and physics. Before quantum mechanics came along and shed light on molecular bonding, no one saw how physics could possibly explain chemical reactions. Now we know better. Perhaps we're in the same boat with consciousness, only the theory that shows how physics explains consciousness hasn't arrived yet.

PONENS: The theory that plays the role quantum mechanics plays in reducing chemistry to physics?

TOLLENS: Yes.

PONENS: Somehow I don't think that's what Joe had in mind.

TOLLENS: Why not? He saw right through our "we got locked in" story, didn't he? Anyway, the view seems reasonable enough to me, whether or not it's Joe's.

PONENS: Sounds more like a cop-out to me. Why couldn't we say the same thing about any difficult philosophical puzzle? Isn't this just an evasion? If my students wrote something like that in a term paper, I'd have them rewrite it and engage with the substantive issues.

TOLLENS: Since when do you have students?

PONENS: Hypothetically.

TOLLENS: I'm not sure the view is a cop-out. You've been going on about how objective science can't explain the relationship between consciousness and the physical world. You think this means we should posit nonphysical properties. Maybe that's the wrong conclusion. Perhaps the source of the problem is ignorance. Maybe there's an unknown type of physical truth: a physical truth that can't be explained in familiar ways.

PONENS: Okay, that's interesting. But I'm not sure it helps. Suppose the source of the problem is ignorance. I don't see why you think that supports physicalism.

TOLLENS: I don't see why not.

PONENS: I know that's what you'd prefer, but the basic thesis here is that we don't know enough about consciousness, the physical, or both to credibly judge how they interrelate. That thesis is neutral on whether physicalism is true or false. It seems disingenuous to say, "We can't know about this stuff—and by the way, it's physical."

TOLLENS: I guess that's right. But there does seem to be some default support for physicalism, if only because in the past physicalism has won similar standoffs.

PONENS: Such as the story you told about chemistry and quantum mechanics?

TOLLENS: Exactly.

PONENS: Yeah, well, I don't buy that analogy. The reason consciousness resists physical explication is unique. So, we shouldn't expect to find close analogies in the history of science.

TOLLENS: I'm getting lost. How does this relate to Joe's view about ignorance?

PONENS: The point is that ignorance is neutral. The hypothesis that we're missing some key pieces of the puzzle doesn't favor either physicalism or anti-physicalism. So can we just forget about Joe?

TOLLENS: Probably not for long. He said he'd be back. Anyway, I think there's a different way to understand what he had in mind.

PONENS: The guy uttered a total of twenty-one words on the subject, and you've got a *third* interpretation?!

TOLLENS: Less is more!

PONENS: Okay, go on if you must.

TOLLENS: Joe said we're wasting our time. Maybe he thought our debate is meaningless.

PONENS: I have little doubt that he did. But then he's the one tilting at air vents.

TOLLENS: No, look, there's a real dilemma here. The question of whether consciousness is physical presupposes that the term "physical" has a definite meaning, right?

PONENS: I suppose, but you know what it means: The physical is what physics talks about and what's implied by physics.

TOLLENS: What do you mean by "physics"? Present-day physics?

PONENS: No, that won't work.

TOLLENS: It sure won't. The laws in current microphysics are probably partly inaccurate and may well be quite far off the mark. And they are almost certainly incomplete.

PONENS: Right. That's why Jackson refers to *completed* physics.

TOLLENS: Ah, that's no solution. What does completed physics look like? We simply don't know. If we take the term "physics" to refer to some future, unspecified theory, then the claim that consciousness is physical will be hopelessly vague. So will the claim that consciousness *isn't* physical.

PONENS: But future physics will be just an improved version of current physics, won't it? If so, then why not let "physical" refer to what's entailed by future physics—or better, by ideal physics?

TOLLENS: In what respects is current physics like ideal physics? Again, there's the vagueness problem.

PONENS: What's wrong with a little vagueness? We're speculating, after all.

TOLLENS: For a start, there's no guarantee that future physics won't go off the rails. Physicists might start concentrating on parapsychology or who knows what. They might start countenancing properties that don't particularly resemble anything found in current physics.

PONENS: I suppose.

TOLLENS: And what if, in a last ditch effort at completeness, physicists start counting phenomenal properties among the fundamental properties? Then the physical truths would *trivially* entail the phenomenal truths. But we wouldn't conclude that physicalism is thereby vindicated. That'd be silly.

PONENS: True again. What's the upshot of all this?

TOLLENS: Think of it as a dilemma.

PONENS: Seems like we've discussed several of those.

TOLLENS: Well, add this one to the list. We could take the term "physical" to refer to what's included in *current* physics or in a future, *ideal* physics. If we go with *current* physics, then it looks as though physicalism is just false—not because of zombies and their ilk, but for straightforward empirical reasons. And if we go with ideal physics, then it looks as though physicalism is hopelessly vague and could even turn out to be trivially true. Either way, there's trouble.

PONENS: Yeah, that's a problem. And I admit I'm not completely sure how to solve it. But that doesn't tempt me to conclude that the debate over physicalism is meaningless. The dilemma is about how we should define the *term* "physical," and that issue isn't central to our debate. The core issue *we've* been discussing is whether phenomenal properties are metaphysically necessitated by the *sorts* of properties we find in science—in current physics, if you like.

TOLLENS: And how do we define *those* properties?

PONENS: I'm not sure, but they all seem to be about structure and dynamics. Let's return to your example of chemistry and quantum mechanics.

TOLLENS: Didn't you say you don't buy that analogy?

PONENS: It makes a nice contrast. Before quantum mechanics, the details of molecular bonding weren't known. But the explanation that was sought, and eventually found, was of a familiar sort: an explanation in terms of structure and dynamics. The same holds true for the explanations we expect from string theory or other developments on the forefront of science. We don't know exactly what we're going to learn from the Large Hadron Accelerator. But we do know the sorts of results to expect, and no such result will explain how consciousness arises from physical processes.

TOLLENS: As far as *you* can tell, monkey-brain.

PONENS: For any hard philosophical problem, it's possible to take the position that we don't know enough to solve it. Or even that we can't solve it, because of our cognitive limitations. I know all about cognitive limitations. I have trouble understanding non-Euclidean geometries, Gödel's incompleteness proof, and certain David Lynch movies. But my contemplation of these things involves a tapering off of my understanding or some sort of confusion. By contrast, I think I understand the type of explanation physics offers reasonably well, even if I don't know the details. And I see pretty clearly that no such explanation will show how the physical truth necessitates the truths about experience.

TOLLENS: You might not see as clearly as you think. Physics might surprise us in what it reveals.

PONENS: And if physics does surprise us, taking into account things other than structure and dynamics, perhaps some headway will be made. But I doubt this will fundamentally change the core issues we've been discussing.

Shouting and clattering are heard in the distance.

TOLLENS: Sounds like Joe found his man.

PONENS: Which means we're next.

TOLLENS: Ah, grand edifice of learning, what a home you have been!

PONENS: Before we go our separate ways, though, I'd like to know where you stand on all this.

TOLLENS: I think you know. I consider the difficulties of integrating nonphysical features into the physical architecture of the world too great to opt for anything but physicalism. That being said, I do admit that the arguments against physicalism have something going for them. In particular, I think I agree with the epistemic step, with one reservation.

PONENS: What's that?

TOLLENS: I agree that there's an epistemic gap for us and for Mary, if Mary is nothing more than an exceptionally smart human being.

PONENS: The epistemic step makes a stronger claim than that.

TOLLENS: Exactly: It says that no pure reasoning can bridge the gap. Not even an ideal reasoner could find any incoherence in the zombie-world hypothesis or deduce what it's like to see red just from the information conveyed to Mary through black-and-white lectures.

PONENS: Right. You reject that stronger claim?

TOLLENS: Not necessarily. I just find it suspicious. I'm concerned that the strong epistemic gap, involving the notion of ideal reasoning, seems compelling only because we conflate it with the weaker epistemic gap, which claims only that creatures like you and me can't deduce the phenomenal from the physical. Also, I'm suspicious of the notion of ideal reasoning in play. But I'm happy to put these concerns aside and suppose the strong epistemic gap exists. I still balk at the inference from that gap to the claim that the physical doesn't metaphysically necessitate the phenomenal.

PONENS: Is that because of the business about phenomenal concepts versus phenomenal properties? Is that your strategy for reconciling physicalism with the epistemic gap?

TOLLENS: I think so. I'd say Mary really does gain information when she leaves the room, and the zombie hypothesis is coherent even on ideal reflection. But all of that can be explained in terms of the distinctive nature of phenomenal concepts and how they differ from physical concepts. Such explanations needn't involve positing nonphysical properties.

PONENS: Okay, but that strategy had problems of its own.

TOLLENS: If I recall, the main objection depends on the assumption that being physical entails being objectively knowable.

PONENS: Right.

TOLLENS: Well, that assumption can be questioned. Physicality and objectivity do seem to be linked, but perhaps this is only because of contingent facts of history. The association has been useful ever since Descartes and other Enlightenment figures emphasized distinctions between objective, physical phenomena and the effects those phenomena have on our minds. Even so, objectivity is an epistemic notion, while physicality ought to be understood as a metaphysical notion. Perhaps some physical properties are irreducibly subjective. Maybe that's the real upshot of the epistemic gap.

PONENS: And what makes those properties physical?

TOLLENS: The idea is that when you fix all of those structural and dynamic truths that you say are the province of physics, the phenomenal properties come for free. It *just is* metaphysically necessary that when things reach a certain level of complexity and have a certain type of organization, there's something it's like to be those things.

PONENS: But the cases we've been discussing—Mary and the zombies—show that the phenomenal truths can't be deduced from the physical truths. And that indicates that the phenomenal truths aren't metaphysically necessitated by the physical truths either.

TOLLENS: How does that follow? Why assume that lack of deductive entailment indicates lack of metaphysical necessitation? Why can't there be metaphysically necessary connections that aren't captured by deductive entailments? If there can, perhaps physical-phenomenal connections are examples.

PONENS: Okay, but what *makes* those connections necessary? You don't want to say that the physical-phenomenal necessities you accept are fundamental truths about the universe, do you?

TOLLENS: Suppose I don't.

PONENS: Then what accounts for those necessary truths? Look, I agree that the connection between deduction and metaphysical necessity may not be as simple and straightforward as I've implied; you're right about that. Nowadays, many philosophers accept metaphysically necessary truths that can't be known simply by reflecting on the associated concepts. A standard example concerns the chemical composition of water. We discovered that water is H_2O empirically, not by deduction. That truth *can't* be discovered just by pure reflection on concepts. Even so, that truth is widely thought to be metaphysically necessary: Any world without H_2O is a world without water.

TOLLENS: Right, and I'm saying that the metaphysically necessary truths to which physicalism is committed are also empirical. But I wouldn't want to make too much of the analogy to water and H_2O.

PONENS: And well you shouldn't.

TOLLENS: No, the word "water" refers to whatever plays a certain functional role: to that which fills our lakes and oceans, runs through faucets, and so on. We can't deduce that H_2O plays that role without empirical investigation. But if we *assume* that H_2O plays that role, then it should be possible to deduce the truth that water is H_2O from the complete physical truth after all. So, we can deduce the necessary truth that water is H_2O from a rich enough story about the physical world.

PONENS: And there's where the analogy breaks down.

TOLLENS: Right, that's what I meant.

PONENS: Good, we're on the same page then. I don't want to belabor the point, but it's important to recognize what the water/H_2O case does and doesn't show. The fact that water is necessarily H_2O doesn't mean that something different from H_2O—something clear and drinkable—couldn't be playing the role we associate with water. In other words, despite the fact that we discovered that our world is one in which H_2O plays that role instead of, say, XYZ, we haven't really changed our minds about what could have been. The space of possibilities is just as we thought it was before we discovered the necessary truth that water is H_2O. It's just that, having discovered that necessary truth, we now know it's strictly incorrect to *describe* the world with XYZ instead of H_2O as one in which water exists.

TOLLENS: Right. So enough already with the lame water/H_2O analogy. I'm not the one who brought it up.

PONENS: I just want you to appreciate that the necessary connections you're embracing are unusual and perhaps even unique. On your view, for example, zombies are metaphysically impossible—any creatures that are just like us physically *must* be just like us phenomenally too—even though the zombie-world scenario is conceptually coherent on ideal reflection. Such necessary truths cry out for explanation.

TOLLENS: Perhaps an explanation could be developed, even if the other models of non-entailment-based necessary truths, such as the water/ H_2O case, don't apply here.

PONENS: Good luck finding one!

TOLLENS: Even if I can't, then we're both guilty of embracing unprecedented discontinuities in nature—and so my situation is no worse than yours. Just a little while ago, you said you want nothing to do with the analogy to chemistry and quantum mechanics because consciousness is unique. And now you're criticizing me for admitting that psychophysical necessities can't be explained along the lines of other widely accepted empirical necessities? Sounds like a double standard.

PONENS: I guess that's fair. But I'm still unclear on your view. Do you think a different explanation for psycho-physical necessities can be found? Or is your view that those necessities are explanatorily brute—that such necessities exist but can't be explained in terms of more fundamental truths?

TOLLENS: I'm not sure. Maybe I should just accept the brute-necessity line. We all have our bullets to bite. Maybe that's mine. Where do your views settle anyway?

PONENS: I wouldn't say they're all that settled. I'd like to take a page from Uncle Joe's "what on Earth do we know?" book. Philosophers and scientists are just beginning to confront the problem of consciousness and its place in nature in relatively systematic ways. We're at the stage where we're just starting to distinguish the hardest problems from others in the vicinity and developing relevant arguments and theories in serious analytical detail. I don't think we should rush to judgment.

TOLLENS: Okay, but don't you have opinions on which view is most promising?

PONENS: I do. I think we should explore alternatives to physicalism.

TOLLENS: Thank you, Captain Obvious. I know you reject physicalism, since you buy the anti-physicalist arguments. I'm asking you one last time: What's your positive view?

PONENS: If I had to place bets, I'd say I'm drawn to the tamer version of the air-duct-guy's view: panprotopsychism. I want to see if the combination problem can be solved, and I don't see why we can't solve it. Maybe a future science of consciousness will include proto-psychophysical laws—laws connecting the protophenomenal and the physical—as part of a fundamental theory. I know that giving up physicalism forces me to accept that states of consciousness end up not causing judgments about those states, at least not in any terribly direct way—and I'm not pleased about that. But I think the benefits of panprotopsychism might outweigh the costs.

Suddenly Joe Epistein appears from between the stacks. His mop is broken, his hair is disheveled, and his elbow is jutting out from a hole in his sleeve.

TOLLENS: I guess you didn't get him.

EPISTEIN: No, I didn't. I've never seen anything like it.

PONENS: Neither have I.

EPISTEIN: So you have seen him?

PONENS: Oops. Just briefly.

EPISTEIN: Well, I might not have flushed him out of the library, but I've got you two. You're not going to give me trouble, are you?

TOLLENS: No sir, we'll go.

EPISTEIN: And I don't want to see you coming back here. Libraries are not hotels. I swear, I'd have thought you would have more sense. Don't you have jobs or anything?

PONENS: Not exactly.

TOLLENS: Speaking of jobs, I don't suppose you need an assistant, do you?

EPISTEIN: Don't even think about it, son. Out you go.

Weary and hungry, Ponens and Tollens walk out of the library to find the day dawning.

TOLLENS: Well, will you look at that! We talked the sun up!

PONENS: So why do I feel like we didn't get anywhere?

TOLLENS: Because you need nourishment, succor.

PONENS: I know a place where they throw out day-old bagels.

TOLLENS: Show me the way.

Reading Suggestions

Monday Night

- A lucid contemporary defense of Cartesian mind-body dualism is W. D. Hart, *The Engines of the Soul* (New York: Cambridge University Press, 1988). Its first three chapters defend a version of Descartes' conceivability argument.
- For much more on the Humean theme of the elusive self, see part III in Derek Parfit, *Reasons and Persons* (New York: Oxford University Press, 1984).
- A helpful discussion of physicalism is Daniel Stoljar, "Physicalism," in the *Stanford Encyclopedia of Philosophy* (http://plato.stanford.edu/entries/physicalism/).
- The causation problem for nonphysical souls is carefully and clearly developed in chapter 3 in Jaegwon Kim, *Physicalism, or Something Near Enough* (Princeton, NJ: Princeton University Press, 2005).

Tuesday Night

- A forceful statement of the view that theories in cognitive science do not solve the hard problem of consciousness is David J. Chalmers, "Facing Up to the Problem of Consciousness," *Journal of Consciousness Studies* 2(3), 1995: 200–19. Chalmers has also written a detailed overview of the literature, "Consciousness and Its Place in Nature," in P. Stich and T. Warfield (eds.), *The Blackwell Guide to the Philosophy of*

Mind (Oxford: Blackwell, 2003). Both are available on his web page (http://consc.net/chalmers/).

- An authoritative discussion of computers and music composition is David Cope, *Computer Models of Musical Creativity* (Cambridge, MA: MIT Press, 2005).
- Classic presentations of the anti-physicalist arguments are Thomas Nagel, "What Is It Like to Be a Bat?," *Philosophical Review* 4, 1974: 435–50; Frank Jackson, "Epiphenomenal Qualia," *Philosophical Quarterly* 32, 1982: 127–36; and lecture III in Saul Kripke, *Naming and Necessity* (Cambridge, MA: Harvard University Press, 1980).
- For a skeptical view about the anti-physicalist arguments from a staunchly physicalist perspective, see chapter 12 in Daniel Dennett, *Consciousness Explained* (Boston: Little, Brown, and Company, 1991).

Wednesday Night

- Papers on the knowledge argument from a wide variety of perspectives have been collected in Peter Ludlow, Yujin Nagasawa, and Daniel Stoljar (eds.), *There's Something about Mary* (Cambridge, MA: MIT Press, 2004).
- A classic presentation of the ability-hypothesis strategy is David Lewis, "What Experience Teaches," in J. Copley-Coltheart (ed.), *Proceedings of the Russellian Society* 13, 1988: 29–57 (Sydney: University of Sydney).
- The acquaintance-hypothesis strategy, a variant of the ability-hypothesis strategy, is proposed in Earl Conee, "Phenomenal Knowledge," *Australasian Journal of Philosophy* 72, 1994: 136–50. This article also presents challenging objections to the ability hypothesis.
- For a balanced critical discussion of the ability-hypothesis strategy, see chapter 1 in Michael Tye, *Consciousness, Color, and Content* (Cambridge, MA: MIT Press, 2000). Chapter 2 in that book presents a provocative argument that the epistemic gap is an illusion, and chapters 3–6 defend and develop representationalism.
- Mary's creator has recently abandoned the knowledge argument and embraced physicalism: Frank Jackson, "Postscript on Qualia," in his *Mind, Method, and Conditionals* (London: Routledge, 1998), 76–79. For an argument that he went astray, see Torin Alter, "Does Representationalism Undermine the Knowledge Argument?," in Torin Alter and Sven Walter (eds.), *Phenomenal Concepts and Phenomenal*

Knowledge: New Essays on Consciousness and Physicalism (New York: Oxford University Press, 2007), 65–76.

Thursday Night

- Superman and Clark Kent battle Mary in Terence Horgan, "Jackson on Physical Information and *Qualia*," *Philosophical Quarterly* 34, 1984: 147–52.
- For the distinction between theoretical and perceptual concepts and its application to Kripke's anti-physicalist argument, see Christopher Hill, "Imaginability, Conceivability, Possibility and the Mind-Body Problem," *Philosophical Studies* 87, 1997: 61–85.
- The classic statement of the phenomenal concepts strategy is Brian Loar, "Phenomenal States," in James Tomberlin (ed.), *Philosophical Perspectives 4: Action Theory and Philosophy of Mind* (Atascadero, CA: Ridgeview, 1990), 81–108. For a more readable presentation of the strategy, based on a different view about phenomenal concepts, see chapters 4–6 in David Papineau, *Thinking about Consciousness* (New York: Oxford University Press, 2002).
- For a forceful challenge to the phenomenal concept strategy, see Daniel Stoljar, "Physicalism and Phenomenal Concepts," *Mind and Language* 20, 2005: 469–94. For another forceful challenge, see David J. Chalmers, "Phenomenal Concepts and the Explanatory Gap," in Alter and Walter, *Phenomenal Concepts and Phenomenal Knowledge,* 167–94.

Friday Night

- A clear discussion of the metaphysics of property dualism and substance dualism is Howard Robinson, "Dualism," in the *Stanford Encyclopedia of Philosophy* (http://plato.stanford.edu/entries/dualism/).
- Jackson created Mary to defend epiphenomenalism. See his "Epiphenomenal Qualia." For more on this view, see William S. Robinson, "Epiphenomenalism," in the *Stanford Encyclopedia of Philosophy* (http://plato.stanford.edu/entries/epiphenomenalism/).
- For descriptions of empirical work on consciousness, see Susan Blackmore, *Consciousness: An Introduction* (New York: Oxford University Press, 2004); and Benjamin Libet, *Mind Time* (Cambridge, MA: Harvard University Press, 2002).

- Chalmers faces up to the paradox of phenomenal judgment in chapter 5 in *The Conscious Mind: In Search of a Fundamental Theory* (New York: Oxford University Press, 1996).
- Nagel flirts with neutral monism in chapter 3 in *The View from Nowhere* (New York: Oxford University Press, 1986).

Saturday

- For clear, precise statements of panpsychism, protopanpsychism, and how these views relate to physicalism, see Chalmers, "Consciousness and Its Place in Nature." The physics-based argument for protopanpsychism originates in Bertrand Russell, *The Analysis of Matter* (London: Kegan Paul, 1927). Galen Strawson presents a provocative argument that we should accept panpsychism because physicalism entails it in "Realistic Monism," in Anthony Freeman (ed.), *Consciousness and Its Place in Nature: Does Physicalism Entail Panpsychism?* (Charlottesville, VA: Imprint Academic, 2006), 3–31.
- The classic statement of the view that we are constitutionally incapable of understanding how brain processes generate experience is Colin McGinn, "Can We Solve the Mind-Body Problem?," *Mind* 98, 1989: 349–66. Daniel Stoljar develops a less skeptical, physicalist version of this approach in *Ignorance and Imagination: The Epistemic Origin of the Problem of Consciousness* (New York: Oxford University Press, 2006).
- A classic statement of the view that the debate over physicalism is literally meaningless is Tim Crane and D. H. Mellor, "There Is No Question of Physicalism," *Mind* 99, 1990: 185–206. A milder and highly readable statement is Barbara Montero, "The Body Problem," *Noûs* 33(3), 1999: 183–20.
- The classic defense of scientific necessities is lecture III in Kripke, *Naming and Necessity.* For an argument against applying Kripke's apparatus to the knowledge argument, see Frank Jackson, "Postscript," in Paul K. Moser and J. K. Trout (eds.), *Contemporary Materialism* (London: Routledge, 1995), 184–89.
- A defense and elaboration of subjective physicalism is Robert Howell, "The Ontology of Subjective Physicalism," forthcoming in *Noûs.*

Sources of Quotations

Page 5: Descartes, R. [1641] *Meditations on First Philosophy.* In Cottingham, J., Stoothoff, R., and Murdoch, D. (eds.), *The Philosophical Writings of Descartes, Volume II.* Cambridge: Cambridge University Press (1984), pp. 3–62: 54.

Page 10: Arnauld, A. [1641] Letter to a Distinguished Gentleman. In Cottingham and Murdoch, *Philosophical Writings of Descartes,* pp. 138–53: 141–42.

Page 12: Hume, D. [1739–40] *A Treatise of Human Nature,* second edition. Oxford: Clarendon Press (1978), p. 634.

Page 29: Jackson, F. What Mary Didn't Know. *Journal of Philosophy* 83 (1986), pp. 291–95: 291.

Page 31: Ibid, p. 293.

Page 74: Nagel, T. *The View from Nowhere.* New York: Oxford University Press (1986), p. 29.

Page 79: Libet, B. *Mind Time.* Cambridge, MA: Harvard University Press (2002), p. 93.

Page 81–82: Chalmers, D. J. *The Conscious Mind: In Search of a Fundamental Theory.* New York: Oxford University Press (1996), p. 180.

Page 87: Lucretius. *On the Nature of the Universe.* Latham, R. E. (trans.). London: Penguin (1999), pp. 61–62.

Page 89: Blackburn, S. Filling in Space. *Analysis* 50 (1990), pp. 60–65: 62–63.

Index